DREAMS IN FOLKLORE

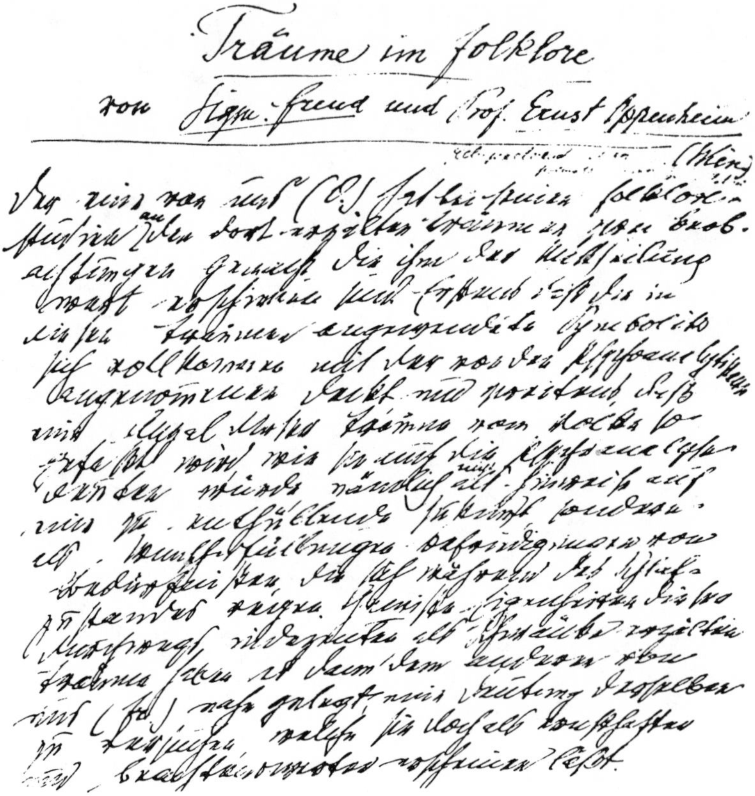
Träume im Folklore
von Sigm. Freud und Prof. Ernst Oppenheim

reproduced from the original manuscript

THE FIRST MANUSCRIPT PAGE OF DREAMS IN FOLKLORE

DREAMS
IN FOLKLORE

BY

SIGMUND FREUD

AND

D. E. OPPENHEIM

Translated from the German
and the Original German Text

INTERNATIONAL UNIVERSITIES PRESS, INC.

Madison   Connecticut

CONTENTS

PREFACE

Sometime in 1909 Professor Ernst Oppenheim, a student of classical mythology and literature, sent Freud the reprint of his article on folklore. It contained references to psychoanalytic observations, and included a dedication to Freud. We infer these facts from Freud's reply to D. E. Oppenheim (see pp. 13-16). Freud thanked Oppenheim and warmly invited him to collaborate in a study of the relationship between folklore and psychoanalysis. Oppenheim accepted this offer of collaboration, as attested by the joint authorship of the *Dreams in Folklore.*

Except for a few short marginal notations and inserts by Oppenheim, the manuscript was entirely handwritten by Freud during the early part of 1911. He used, in addition, typescript material presumably furnished by Oppenheim, which Freud inserted in the appropriate places in the text. Strachey, in the Editor's Note regarding the English translation, discusses in detail the respective contributions to the manuscript of each author. After Freud prepared the manuscript, which consists of 24 large, 10 x 15, sheets, he left it in the

[7]

possession of Oppenheim for his comments. Shortly thereafter, Oppenheim dissociated himself from Freud and the Vienna Psychoanalytical Society, and presumably never returned the manuscript to Freud, never published it, and, so far as we know, never made its contents public. There is no direct reference by Freud to this paper in his published writings, nor in the psychoanalytic literature, although Ernst Kris* as well as Strachey note that Freud made a reference to Oppenheim's interest in folklore dreams in a footnote contained only in the 1911 edition of *The Interpretation of Dreams.*

So far as is known, *Dreams in Folklore* is the only unpublished Freud paper of any significant length, and with a few exceptions** is the only original manuscript Freud wrote prior to 1914 which is preserved, all the others having been destroyed by him when he moved his office.

I first became aware of the existence of this manuscript about five years ago when Dr. Jacob Shatzky, formerly Chief Librarian at the New York State Psychiatric Institute, informed me that he knew of the existence of an "unknown" and unpublished early Freud paper which was not in

---

* Personal Communication.
** The papers published in *Schriften aus dem Nachlass.* Volume XVII of *Gesammelte Werke.*

England nor in the possession of the Freud family, and which he was in the process of acquiring. I would assume he had reference to *Folklore in Dreams*. However, several analysts, including Dr. Ernst Kris, had known of the existence of this manuscript for a number of years, but were unaware of its location, and uncertain as to the exact contents. Dr. K. R. Eissler ultimately discovered the location of the manuscript which was in the possession of Oppenheim's daughter, Mrs. Liffman, who was living in Australia, and had obtained it after the death of her parents. Mrs. Liffman arranged, through the services of a New York dealer of rare books and manuscripts, to have the manuscript sent to New York, where, with the invaluable assistance of Dr. Eissler, we were able to acquire the paper for the Freud Archives.

The first presentation of *Folklore in Dreams* before a psychoanalytic group was at the Annual Meeting of the American Psychoanalytic Association in Chicago in May, 1957, where a summary of its contents was read. The full text of the manuscript and of Freud's letter to Oppenheim are published here for the first time.

The German version of the manuscript is printed exactly as originally written by Freud. A few errors in spelling in addition to some wrong references, which Freud undoubtedly would have

[9]

corrected prior to publication, are therefore left intact. In the English version, however, these errors have been corrected by Mr. Strachey.

Parts of the manuscript and particularly some of the pencilled marginal notes, which had partially faded, were difficult to "decipher." We are indebted to Mrs. Eva J. Meyer, Librarian of the New York Psychoanalytic Institute, for her very helpful assistance in these matters, in addition to the preparation of the German typescript from the original writing.

We are very grateful to Mr. Strachey for his supervision of the English translation of the paper which was done by A. M. O. Richards, and for the thoroughness of his research in determining the approximate date of the *Folklore in Dreams,* in addition to other pertinent details about the manuscript and Professor Ernst Oppenheim.

Freud's introductory and concluding paragraphs clearly indicate the essential theme of the paper. However, an interesting sidelight is given into Freud's character: he reveals himself here as being deeply sympathetic to the problems of the "common man." He comments that the folklore tales of dreams are frequently obscene dreams which are always told humorously. But then, he adds, "it is doing the common people an injustice to assume that they employ this form of entertainment merely to satisfy the coarsest desires. It seems rather that behind these ugly façades are concealed mental reactions to impressions of life which are to be taken seriously, which even strike a sad note —reactions to which common people are ready to surrender, but only if they are accompanied by a yield of coarse pleasure."

Bernard L. Pacella, M.D.

PROF. DR. FREUD   19 Berggasse
                                   Vienna, IX
                                   October 28, 1909

Dear Dr. Oppenheim,

The paper you send me has taken me by sur-
prise. Several passages in it which you have under-
lined recall things that are familiar to me; and,
apart from that, it makes me regret once again—
as I have so often done before—that so little has
been added to my knowledge of antiquity since my
schooldays. The dedication, too, which you have
added to the offprint strikes me as of the greatest
significance. Do not be astonished, then, if my
curiosity leads me to enquire how I have come by
the honor you have shown me, and whether I may
recognize in you a reader of my works who, behind all my different writings, has divined their
deeper sense.

I have long been haunted by the idea that our
studies on the content of the neuroses might be
destined to solve the riddle of the formation of
myths, and that the nucleus of mythology is noth-

ing other than what we speak of as "the nuclear complex of the neuroses"—as I was able not long since to bring it to light in the "Analysis of a Phobia in a Five-Year-Old Boy." Two of my pupils, Abraham in Berlin and Otto Rank in Vienna, have ventured upon an attempt to invade the territory of mythology and to make conquests in it with the help of the technique of psychoanalysis and its angle of approach. But we are amateurs, and have every reason to be afraid of mistakes. We are lacking in academic training and familiarity with the material. Thus we are looking about for an enquirer whose development has been in the reverse direction, who possesses the specialized knowledge and is ready to apply to it the psychoanalytic armory that we will gladly put at his command—a native enquirer, as one might say, who will be able to achieve something quite other than we who are intruders of another species.

Can it be that you are willing to be this man we are longing for? What do you know of psychoanalysis? And have you the leisure and inclination to plunge into it more deeply for these ends? Forgive me if I am mistaken and have interpreted the signs too far.

Looking forward to hearing from you,

I am very sincerely yours,

Freud

BRIEF VON SIGMUND FREUD AN D. E. OPPENHEIM

PROF. DR. FREUD   *28. Okt. 09*
                        Wien, IX. Berggasse 19.
    Sehr geehrter Herr Doktor,
Sie überraschen mich mit einer Zusendung, in
welcher mehrere angestrichene Stellen an mir bekannte Dinge anklingen, und die mich sonst von
neuem—wie so oft—bedauern lässt, dass zu
meiner Kenntnis der Alten seit den Gymnasial-
zeiten so wenig hinzugekommen ist. Sie versehen
den Abdruck mit einer Widmung, die ich als
höchst bedeutsam noch erkenne. Wundern Sie
sich also nicht, wenn ich neugierig anfrage, wie ich
zu der mir erwiesenen Ehrung gekommen bin,
und ob ich einen Leser meiner Arbeiten in Ihnen
erkennen darf, der durch alles Einzelwerk hindurch den tieferen Sinn derselben erraten hat?
    Seit längerer Zeit verfolgt mich die Idee, dass
unsere Studien über den Inhalt der Neurosen berufen sein könnten, die Rätsel der Mythenbildung
aufzuklären, und dass der Kern der Mythologie

kein anderer ist, als was wir den "Kernkomplex
der Neurose" nennen, wie ich ihn unlängst in der
Analyse der Phobie eines fünfjährigen Knaben
blosslegen konnte. Zwei meiner Schüler, Abraham
in Berlin u. O. Rank in Wien haben den Versuch
gewagt ins mythologische Gebiet einzufallen und
dort mit Hilfe der psychoanalytischen Technik
und Gesichtspunkte Eroberungen zu machen.
Aber wir sind Dilettanten und haben allen Grund,
uns vor Irrtümern zu fürchten. Uns fehlt der
Schulsack. Die Vertrautheit mit dem Material.
Wir schauen darum nach einem Forscher aus, der
die umgekehrte Entwicklung genommen hat, der
die Sachkenntnis besitzt und unser psychoana-
lytisches Rüstzeug, das wir ihm gerne zur Verfü-
gung stellen, dazu annehmen will, einen einge-
borenen Forscher sozusagen, der ganz anderes
wird leisten können als die ortfremden Eindring-
linge.

Sollten Sie dieser ersehnte Mann sein wollen?
Was wissen Sie von der Psychoanalyse? Und haben
Sie Musse und Neigung zu dem angegebenen
Zwecke weiter in sie einzudringen?

Verzeihen Sie, wenn ich mich geirrt und
Zeichen überdeutet habe.

In der Erwartung von Ihnen zu hören,

Ihr in Hochachtung ergebener

Freud

28 Okt 09

PROF. Dr. FREUD

WIEN, IX. BERGGASSE 19.

Sehr geehrter Herr Doktor

Sie überraschen mich mit einer Zusendung, in welcher an mehreren ausgezeichneten Stellen an mich bekannte Dinge anklingen, und die mich doch von Neuem mir so oft bedauern läßt, daß zu meiner Kenntnis der Alten seit der Gymnasialzeit so wenig hinzugekommen ist. Sie versehen das Exemplar mit einer Widmung, die ich als höchst bedeutsam anerkennen. Wundern Sie sich also nicht, wenn ich neugierig anfrage, wie ich zu der mich auszeichnenden Schickung gekommen bin und ob ich einen Leser meiner Arbeiten in Ihnen erkennen darf, der durch alles Fragwürdige hindurch den einfachen Sinn derselben erraten hat?

Seit längerer Zeit verfolgt mich die Idee, daß unsere Studien über den Inhalt der Neurosen berufen sein könnten, die Rätsel der Mythenbildung aufzuklären, und daß der Kern der Mythologie kein anderer ist, als was wir den „Kernkomplex der Neurose" nennen, wie ich ihn vor kürzlich in der Analyse der Phobie eines fünfjährigen Knaben bloßlegen konnte. Zwei meiner Schüler, Abraham in Berlin u. O. Rank in Wien haben den Versuch gewagt, ins mythologische Gebiet einzufallen und dort mit Hilfe der psychoanalytischen Technik und Gesichtspunkte Eroberungen zu machen. Aber wir sind Dilettanten und haben allen Grund, uns vor Irrtümern zu fürchten. Uns fehlt das Schulgerät.

die Brolsamhuf mit dem Material das schaaen
dasim nach einem gosspos und das du nugstshu
funmittung genommen sit beg du ...
... und mehr ...
mit du geaus ... stallen ...
... will, ...
... aubonos ...
...

... du ...
... du von das ...
... Naignig, ...
...

... du venn ich nich ...
... übereilat hebe.

In der ... von Ihnen zu hören,
Ihr in Hochachtung ergebener

Freud

PART I

DREAMS IN FOLKLORE

by

SIGMUND FREUD

and

D. E. OPPENHEIM

Translated from the original German
by
A. M. O. RICHARDS

Edited with an Introduction
by
JAMES STRACHEY

EDITOR'S INTRODUCTION

The existence of this paper, written jointly by Freud and Professor D. E. Oppenheim of Vienna, had been totally overlooked until the summer of 1956, when Mrs. Liffman, Oppenheim's daughter, then living in Australia, brought it to the notice of a New York bookseller. Soon afterwards the manuscript was acquired on behalf of the Sigmund Freud Archives by Dr. Bernard L. Pacella, and it is through his generosity, and with the unfailing help of Dr. K. R. Eissler, the Secretary of the Archives, that we are now able to publish it for the first time. The German original is included in this volume.

David Ernst Oppenheim, Freud's collaborator in this paper, was born at Brünn, in what is now Czechoslovakia, in 1881. He was a classical scholar and became professor at the Akademisches Gymnasium in Vienna, where he taught Greek and Latin. Dr. Ernest Jones (*Sigmund Freud: Life and Work,* Vol. II) mentions him among those who attended Freud's University lectures in 1906; but his acquaintance with Freud apparently dates only from 1909. In the autumn of that year he seems to have sent Freud a copy of a paper dealing with classical mythology in a way which showed a knowledge of psychoanalytic literature, for a letter of Freud's has survived (dated October 28, 1909) thanking him for it in very warm terms and suggesting that he should bring his knowledge of the classics into the service of psychoanalytic studies.[1] The outcome was evidently his association with the Vienna Psychoanalytic Society, of which (again according to Jones, *loc. cit.*) he became a member in 1910. On April 20 of that year he opened a symposium in the Vienna Society on suicide (particularly among schoolboys), which was published in the form of a brochure (1910). Oppenheim's contribution will be found there under the signature "Unus Multorum," but it was reprinted under his own name some years later in a collective work *Heilen und Bilden,* edited by Adler and Furtmüller (1914). The published minutes of the Vienna Society show that he read three "short communications" during 1910 and 1911, the first of which, on "Folklore Material Bearing upon Dream Symbolism" (November 16, 1910) has an evident relation to the present work. In the spring of 1911 Freud brought out the third edition of *The Interpretation of Dreams* and in this he

---

[1] See pp. 13-16.

inserted a footnote at the very end of the book, mentioning Oppenheim's work in connection with dreams in folklore and stating that a paper on the subject was shortly to appear *(Standard Ed., 5,* 621). The footnote was omitted in all later editions. This omission, as well as the disappearance of the present paper, is no doubt accounted for by the fact that soon afterwards Oppenheim became an adherent of Adler's and, along with five other members, resigned from the Vienna Psychoanalytic Society on October 11, 1911. He died during the second World War in the concentration camp at Theresienstadt, in which both he and his wife were interned. After the war his wife emigrated to Australia, taking with her the manuscript, which she had been able to preserve. In accordance with her wishes, its publication was withheld until after her own death.

It is possible to date Freud's share in this paper within fairly narrow limits. It cannot have been written before the early part of 1911, as is shown by a reference in it to Stekel's *Die Sprache des Traumes* which was published toward the beginning of that year (p. 49); and it must have been completed before the final breach with Adler the same summer.

Though the manuscript as we now possess it has had no final revision by its authors, it in fact calls for very little editorial tidying up, and it gives us a clear means of judging the share taken in it by its two authors. The raw material was evidently collected by Oppenheim. This was largely derived from the periodical *Anthropophyteia* (Leipzig, 1904-1913), edited by F. S. Krauss, in which Freud had always taken a special interest.[2] (Cf. his open letter to its editor, 1910, and his preface to Bourke's *Scatalogic Rites of All Nations*, 1913, which is particularly relevant to the present paper.) Oppenheim copied out this material, partly in typescript and partly by hand (adding a very few short remarks), and submitted it to Freud, who then arranged it in an appropriate sequence, pasted Oppenheim's sheets on to much larger sheets of his own, and interpolated them with a profuse commentary. Freud must then have returned the whole manuscript to Oppenheim, who seems once more to have added two or three further notes (some of them in shorthand).

In the version printed below, therefore, the contributions made by the two authors are automatically distinguished, if we leave out of account any previous interchange of views. All the "raw material," printed here in somewhat smaller type, is

---

[2] Some of the material is also taken from *Kryptadia,* a similar periodical published in Heilbronn and Paris between 1883 and 1911.

to be attributed to Oppenheim; Freud is responsible for everything else—the introduction, the commentaries, the conclusion, and the whole arrangement of the material. The only change made by the editor has been to transfer the references from the body of the text to the footnotes. Oppenheim's very few marginal remarks have also been printed as footnotes, with their authorship specified. Some of these, however, have unfortunately become illegible.

No attempt has been made in the translation to reproduce the various dialects in which many of the original stories are written. A conventional idiom has been adopted, of a kind usually associated with folk tales. The references have been checked wherever possible, and a number of errors in them corrected. Editorial comments are printed in square brackets.

J. S.

DREAMS
IN FOLKLORE

"CELSI PRAETEREUNT AUSTERA POEMATA RAMNES."
PERSIUS, *Satirae*[1]

One of us (O.) in his studies of folklore has made two observations with regard to the dreams narrated there which seem to him worth communicating. Firstly, that the symbolism employed in these dreams coincides completely with that accepted by psychoanalysis, and secondly, that a number of these dreams are understood by the common people in the same way as they would be interpreted by psychoanalysis—that is, not as premonitions about a still unrevealed future, but as the fulfillment of wishes, the satisfaction of needs which arise during the state of sleep. Certain peculiarities of these, usually indecent, dreams, which are told as comic anecdotes, have encouraged the second of us (Fr.) to attempt an interpretation of them which has made them seem more serious and more deserving of attention.

---

[1] [The motto at the head of the work is in Oppenheim's writing. The quotation is actually line 342 of Horace's *Ars Poetica*. The precise sense of the words is disputed by the experts, but its application here may be paraphrased: "Haughty persons in authority disdain poems that are lacking in charm."]

I

PENIS SYMBOLISM IN DREAMS OCCURRING IN FOLKLORE

The dream which we introduce first, although it contains no symbolic representations, sounds almost like ridicule of the prophetic and a plea in favor of the psychological interpretation of dreams.

A Dream Interpretation[2]

A girl got up from her bed and told her mother that she had had a most strange dream.

"Well, what did you dream, then?" asked her mother.

"How shall I tell you? I don't know myself what it was—some sort of long and red and blunted thing."

"Long means a road," said her mother reflectively, "a long road; red means joy, but I don't know what blunted can mean."

The girl's father, who was getting dressed meanwhile, and was listening to everything that the mother and daughter were saying, muttered at this, more or less to himself: "It sounds rather like my cock."[3]

---

[2] "Südslavische Volksüberlieferungen, die sich auf den Geschlechtsverkehr beziehen [Southern Slav Folk Traditions Concerning Sexual Intercourse]," collected and elucidated by F. S. Krauss, *Anthropophyteia*, 7, 450, No. 820.

[3] [*Addition by* F. S. Krauss:] See *Anthropophyteia*, *1*, 4, No. 5. Cf. further the German Jewish proverb: "The goose dreams of maize and the betrothed girl of a prick." [See also *The Interpretation of Dreams, Standard Ed., 4*, 131-132.]

It is very much more convenient to study dream symbolism in folklore than in actual dreams. Dreams are obliged to conceal things and only surrender their secrets to interpretation; these comic anecdotes, however, which are disguised as dreams, are intended as communications, meant to give pleasure to the person who tells them as well as to the listener, and therefore the interpretation is added quite unashamedly to the symbol. These stories delight in stripping off the veiling symbols.

In the following quatrain the penis appears as a scepter:

> Last night I dreamt
> I was King of the land,
> And how jolly I was
> With a prick in my hand.[4]

Now compare with this "dream" the following examples in which the same symbolism is employed outside a dream.

> I love a little lass
> The prettiest I've seen,
> I'll put a scepter in your hand
> And you shall be a queen.[5]

---

[4] "Niederösterreichische [Lower Austrian] Schnadahüpfeln," collected by Dr. H. Rollett. [The *Schnadahüpfel* is a light-hearted extempore verse in four lines, the second and fourth lines rhyming, sung in Bavarian and Austrian mountain districts.] *Anthropophyteia, 5,* 151, No. 2.

[5] From the Austrian Alps, *Kryptadia, 4,* 111, No. 160.

"Remember, my boy," said Napoleon,
The Emperor of renown,
"So long as the prick is the scepter
The cunt will be the crown."[6]

A different variant of this symbolic exaltation of the genitals is favored in the imagination of artists. A fine etching by Félicien Rops,[7] bearing the title *"Tout est grand chez les rois"* ["Everything about kings is great"], shows the naked figure of a king with the features of the *Roi Soleil* [Louis XIV], whose gigantic penis, which rises to arm level, itself wears a crown. The right hand balances a scepter, while the left clasps a large orb, which by reason of a central cleft achieves an unmistakable resemblance to another part of the body which is the object of erotic desires.[8] The index finger of the left hand is inserted into this groove.

In the Silesian folksong that follows, the dream is only invented in order to hide a different occur-

---

[6] From Gaming in Lower Austria, *Anthropophyteia, 3,* 190, No. 85, 4.

[7] *Das erotische Werk des Félicien Rops:* 42 Etchings. Privately printed, 1905. Plate 20.

[8] [*Marginal Note by* Oppenheim:] Like the orb in Rops's picture, a Roman relief in the Amphitheatre at Nîmes shows an egg transformed into a symbol of the female sexual organs by means of a similar groove. Here, too, the male counterpart is not absent. It appears as a phallus strangely furbished up as a bird which sits on four eggs of the kind described—one might say brooding them. [The reference added is untraceable].

rence. The penis appears here as a *worm* ("fat earthworm"), which has crawled into the girl, and at the right time crawls out again as a *little worm* (baby).[9]

SONG OF THE EARTHWORM[10]

Asleep on the grass one day a young lass
Susanna of passion was dreaming,
A soft smile did play around her nose as she lay
While she thought of her swain and his scheming.

Then—dream full of fear!—it swift did appear
That her lover so handsome and charming
Had become as she slept a fat earthworm which crept
Right inside. What could be more alarming?

Full of dread in her heart she awoke with a start
And swift to the village she hied her
And tearfully told all the folk young and old
That an earthworm had crawled up inside her.

Her wailing and tears came at last to the ears
Of her mother who cursed and swore roundly;
With bodings of gloom she repaired to her room
And examined the maiden most soundly.

For the earthworm she sought, but alas! could find
  nought—
An unfortunate thing which dismayed her.
So she hurried away without further delay
To ask the wise woman to aid her.

---

[9] [*"Würmchen"* ("little worm") is a common German expression for "baby."]

[10] "Schlesische Volkslieder [Silesian Folksongs]," transcribed by Dr. von Waldheim, *Anthropophyteia*, 7, 369.

With cunning she laid out the cards for the maid
And said: "We must wait a while longer.
"I have questioned the Knave, but no answer he gave;
"Perhaps the Red King will prove stronger.

" 'Tis the news that you fear which the Red King
    speaks clear:
"The worm really crawled in the girlie;
"But as everything bides its due times and its tides
"To catch it 'tis yet much too early."

When Susanna had heard the lugubrious word
She went to her chamber full sadly;
Till at last there appeared the dread hour that she
    feared
And out crept the little worm gladly.

So be warned, every lass: do not dream on the grass,
But let poor Susanna's fate guide you,
Or—as you too may know, to your grief and your
    woe—
A fat earthworm will creep up inside you.[11]

The same symbolization of the penis as a *worm*
is familiar from numerous obscene jokes.

The dream which now follows symbolizes the
penis as a *dagger:* the woman who dreams it is
pulling at a dagger in order to stab herself, when

---

[11] [*Footnote by* F. S. Krauss:] Cf. p. 359 and the Southern
Slav versions in Krauss, "Die Zeugung in Sitte, Brauch und
Glauben der Südslaven" ["Procreation in the Customs, Usages
and Beliefs of the Southern Slavs"], *Kryptadia, 6,* 259-269
and 375 f.

she is awakened by her husband and exhorted not to tear his member off.

A Bad Dream[12]

A woman dreamt that things had got to such a pitch that they had nothing to eat before the holiday and could not buy anything either. Her husband had drunk up all the money. There was only a lottery ticket left and even this they really ought to pawn. But the man was still keeping it back, for the draw was to be on the second of January. He said: "Wife, now tomorrow is the draw, let the ticket wait a while longer. If we don't win, then we must sell the ticket or pawn it."—"Well, the devil take it, all you've bought is worry, and you've got about as much out of it as there is milk in a billy-goat." So the next day arrived. See, along came the newspaper man. He stopped him, took a copy and began to look down the list. He ran his eyes over the figures, he looked through every column, his number was not among them. He did not trust his eyes, looked through once again and this time sure enough he came upon the number of his ticket. The number was the same, but the number of the series did not fit. Once again he did not trust himself and thought to himself: "This must be a mistake. Wait a bit, I will go to the bank and make certain one way or the other." So he went there with his head hanging. On the way he met a second news-

---

[12] [Tarasevsky, *Das Geschlechtsleben des Ukrainischen Bauernvolkes (The Sexual Life of the Ukrainian Peasants)*, Leipzig, 1909, 289, No. 265.]

paper man. He bought another copy of a second
paper, scanned the list and found the number of his
ticket straight away. The number of the series, too,
was the same as the one which included his ticket.
The prize of 5,000 roubles fell to his lot. He burst
into the bank, rushed up and asked them to pay out
on the winning ticket at once. The banker said that
they could not pay out yet, only in a week or two. He
began to beg and pray: "Please be kind, give me
1,000 at least, I can get the rest later!" The banker
refused, but advised him to apply to the private in-
dividual who had procured the winning lottery ticket
for him. What was to be done now? Just then a little
Jew appeared as though he had sprung up from the
ground. He smelt a bargain and made him an offer
to pay over the money at once, though instead of
5,000 only 4,000. The fifth thousand would be his
own share. The man was delighted at this good
fortune and decided to give the Jew the thousand,
just so that he could get the money on the spot. He
took the money from the Jew and handed over the
ticket to him. Then he went home. On the way he
went into an inn, swallowed a quick glass and from
there went straight home. He walked along grinning
and humming a little song. His wife saw him through
the window and thought: "Now he's certainly sold
the lottery ticket; you can see he's cheerful, he's probably paid a visit to the inn and got himself drunk
because he was feeling miserable." Then he came in-
doors, put the money on the kitchen table and went
to his wife to bring her the good news that he had
won and had got the money. While they were hugging

and kissing one another to their heart's content because they were so happy, their little three-year-old daughter grabbed the money and threw it into the stove. Then they came along to count the money and it was no longer there. The last bundle of notes was already on fire. In a rage the man seized hold of the little girl by the legs and dashed her against the stove. She dropped dead. Disaster stared him in the face, there was no escaping Siberia now. He seized his revolver and bang! he shot himself in the chest and dropped dead. Horrified by such a disaster, the woman snatched up a dagger and was going to stab herself. She tried to pull it out of the sheath but could not manage it however she tried. Then she heard a voice as though from Heaven: "Enough, let go! What are you doing?" She woke up and saw that she was not pulling at a dagger but at her husband's tool, and he was saying: "Enough, let go or you'll tear it off!"

The representation of the penis as a weapon, cutting knife,[13] dagger, etc., is familiar to us from the anxiety dreams of abstinent women in particular and also lies at the root of numerous phobias in neurotic people. The complicated dis-

---

[13] [*Footnote by* Oppenheim:] A knife is habitually carried by a burglar ["*Einbrecher,*" literally: "someone who breaks in"]. The kind of breaking in intended is shown by a proverbial phrase from Solingen [in the industrial Rhineland], reported in *Anthropophyteia, 5,* 182 [No. 11]: "After marriage comes a burglary [breaking in]." Cf. the Berlin slang term "*Brecheisen*" ["jemmy," literally, "breaking iron"] for "a powerful penis" (*Anthropophyteia, 7, 33*).

guise of this present dream, however, demands that we should make an attempt to clarify our understanding of it by a psychoanalytic interpretation based on interpretations already carried out. In doing so we are not overlooking the fact that we shall be going beyond the material presented in the folk tale itself and that consequently our conclusions will lose in certainty.

Since this dream ends in an act of sexual aggression carried out by the woman as a dream action,[14] this suggests that we should take the state of *material* need in the content of the dream as a substitute for a state of *sexual* need. Only the most extreme libidinal compulsion can at all justify such aggressiveness on the part of a woman. Other pieces of the dream content point in a quite definite and different direction. The blame for this state of need is ascribed to the man. (He had drunk up all the money.)[15] The dream goes on to get rid of the man and the child and skillfully evades the sense of guilt attached to these wishes

---

[14] [*"Traumhandlung."* This term is used in the present paper to describe an action which is carried out by someone in a dream but is at the same time a real action. The concept appears not to be discussed in *The Interpretation of Dreams*.]

[15] [*Marginal Note by* Oppenheim:] Cf. further below our remarks on "marriage portion" as a term for "penis" and "purse" for "testes" and also comparisons between virility and wealth and between the thirst for gold and libido. [It is not clear to what remarks this reference is intended to apply.]

by causing the child to be killed by the man who then commits suicide out of remorse. Since this is the content of the dream we are led to conclude from many analogous instances that here is a woman who is not satisfied by her husband and who in her fantasies is longing for another marriage. It is all one for the interpretation whether we like to regard this dissatisfaction of the dreamer's as a permanent state of want or merely as the expression of a temporary one. The lottery, which in the dream brought about a short-lived state of happiness, could perhaps be understood as a symbolic reference to marriage. This symbol has not yet been identified with certainty in psychoanalytic work, but people are in the habit of saying that marriage is a game of chance, that in marriage one either draws the winning lot or a blank.[16] The numbers, which have been enormously magnified[17] by the dream work, could well correspond in that case to the number of repetitions of the satisfying act that are wished for. We are thus made aware that the act of pulling the man's member not only has the meaning of libidinal provocation but also the additional meaning of con-

---

[16] Another dream about a lottery in this little collection confirms this suggestion. [See p. 63 below.]

[17] Psychoanalytic experience shows that noughts appended to numbers in dreams can be ignored in interpretation.

temptuous criticism, as though the woman wanted to pull the member off—as the man correctly assumed—because it was no good, did not fulfill its obligations.

We should not have lingered over the interpretation of this dream and exploited it beyond its overt symbolism were it not that other dreams which likewise end in a dream action demonstrate that the common people have recognized here a typical situation that which, wherever it occurs, is susceptible to the same explanation. (Cf. below [p. 57].)

II

FECES SYMBOLISM AND RELATED DREAM ACTIONS

Psychoanalysis has taught us that in the very earliest period of childhood feces is a highly prized substance, in relation to which coprophilic instincts find satisfaction. With the repression of these instincts, which is accelerated as much as possible by upbringing, this substance falls into contempt and then serves conscious purposes as a means of expressing disdain and scorn. Certain forms of mental activity such as joking are still able to make the obstructed source of pleasure accessible for a brief moment, and thus show how much of the esteem in which human beings once held their feces still remains preserved in the unconscious. The most important residue of this former esteem is, however, that all the interest which the child has had in feces is transferred in the adult onto another material which he learns in life to set above almost everything else—gold.[1] How old this connection between excrement and gold is can be seen from an observation by Jeremias:[2] gold, according to ancient oriental mythology, is the excrement of hell.[3]

In dreams in folklore gold is seen in the most unambiguous way to be a symbol of feces. If the sleeper feels a need to defecate, he dreams of gold, of treasure. The disguise in the dream, which is designed to mislead him into satisfying his need in bed, usually makes the pile of feces serve as a sign to mark the place where the treasure is to be found; that is to say, the dream—as though by means of endopsychic perception—states outright, even if in a reversed form, that gold is a sign or a symbol for feces.

A simple treasure or defecation dream of this kind is the following one, related in the *Facetiae* of Poggio.

---

[1] Cf. "Character and Anal Erotism" (1908). [Freud, *Standard Ed., 9*.]

[2] Alfred Jeremias, *Das alte Testament im Lichte des alten Orients,* Leipzig, 1904, 115*n.*

[3] [*Marginal Note by* Oppenheim:] Similarly in Mexico.

[37]

DREAM GOLD[4]

A certain man related in company that he dreamt he had found gold. Thereupon another man capped it with this story. (What follows is quoted verbatim.)

"My neighbor once dreamt that the Devil had led him to a field to dig for gold; but he found none. Then the Devil said: 'It is there for sure, only you cannot dig it up now; but take note of the place so that you may recognize it again by yourself.'

"When the man asked that the place should be made recognizable by some sign, the Devil suggested: 'Just shit on it, then it will not occur to anybody that there is gold lying hidden here and you will be able to recognize the exact place.' The man did so and then immediately awoke and felt that he had done a great heap in his bed."

(We give the conclusion in summary.) As he was fleeing from the house, he put on a cap in which a cat had done its business during the same night. He had to wash his head and his hair. "Thus his dream gold was turned to filth."

Tarasevsky (*op. cit.,* 194, No. 232) reports a similar dream from the Ukraine in which a peasant receives some treasure from the Devil, to whom he has lit a candle, and puts a pile of feces to mark the place.[5]

We need not be surprised if the Devil appears

---

[4] Poggio [Bracciolini], *Facetiae,* No. 130. [As will be seen, the anecdote has been slightly abbreviated by Oppenheim.]

[5] [*Addition by* Oppenheim:] Attention is there drawn to parallels in *Anthropophyteia, 4,* 342-345, Nos. 580-581.

in these two dreams as a bestower of treasure and a seducer, for the Devil—himself an angel expelled from Paradise—is certainly nothing else than the personification of the repressed unconscious instinctual life.[6]

The motives behind these simple comic anecdotes about dreams appear to be exhausted in a cynical delight in dirt and a malicious satisfaction over the dreamer's embarrassment. But in other dreams about treasures the form taken by the dream is confused in all sorts of ways and includes various constituents the origin and significance of which we may well investigate. For we shall not regard even these dream contents, which are intended to provide a rationalistic justification for obtaining the satisfaction, as entirely arbitrary and meaningless.

In the two next examples, the dream is not ascribed to a person sleeping alone but to one of two sleepers—two men—who share a bed. As a result of the dream, the dreamer dirties his bedfellow.

---

[6] "Character and Anal Erotism" (1908).

A LIVELY DREAM[7]

Two traveling journeymen arrived weary at an inn and asked for a night's lodging. "Yes," said the host, "if you are not afraid, you can have a bedroom, but it's a haunted one. If you want to stay, that's all right, and the night will cost you nothing as far as sleeping goes." The lads asked one another: "Are you frightened?"—"No." Very well, so they seized another liter of wine and went to the room assigned to them.

They had hardly been lying down any time when the door opened and a white figure glided through the room. One fellow said to the other: "Didn't you see something?" "Yes." "Well, why didn't you say anything?" "Just wait, it's going to come through the room again." Sure enough, the figure glided in again. One of the lads jumped up swiftly, but swifter still the ghost glided out through the crack in the door. The lad, by no means slow, pulled open the door and saw the figure, a beautiful woman, already half way down the stairs. "What are you doing there?" the lad shouted out. The figure stood still, turned round and spoke: "Now I am released. I have long had to wander. As a reward take the treasure which lies just at the spot where you are standing." The lad was as much frightened as delighted, and in order to mark the place he lifted up his shirt and planted a fine pile, for he thought that no one would

[7] F. Wernert, "Deutsche Bauernerzählungen gesammelt im Ober- und Unterelsass [German Peasant Tales, Collected in Upper and Lower Alsace]," *Anthropophyteia, 3,* 72, No. 15.

[40]

wipe out that mark. But just as he was at his happiest, he felt someone suddenly seize hold of him. "You dirty swine," someone bellowed in his ear, "you're shitting on my shirt." At these coarse words the happy dreamer awoke from his fairy tale good fortune to find himself roughly hurled out of bed.

HE SHAT ON THE GRAVE[8]

Two gentlemen arrived at a hotel, ate their evening meal and drank and at last wanted to go to bed. They asked the host if he would show them to a room. As the rooms were all occupied the host gave up his own bed to them, which they were both to sleep in, and he would soon find a place for himself to sleep somewhere else. The two men lay down in the same bed. A spirit appeared to one of them in a dream, lit a candle and led him to the churchyard. The lychgate opened and the spirit with the candle in its hand and the man behind him walked up to the grave of a maiden. When they had reached the grave, the candle suddenly went out. "What shall I do now? How shall I tell which is the maiden's grave tomorrow, when it is day?" he asked in the dream. Then an idea came to his rescue, he pulled down his drawers and shat on the grave. When he had finished shitting, his comrade, who was sleeping beside him, struck him first on one cheek and then on the other: "What! You'd shit right in my face?"

---

[8] [F. S. Krauss, "Südslavische Volksüberlieferungen, die sich auf den Geschlechtsverkehr beziehen (Southern Slav Folk Traditions Concerning Sexual Intercourse)," *Anthropophyteia, 5,* 346, No. 737.]

In these two dreams, in place of the Devil other supernatural figures appear, namely, ghosts—that is, spirits of dead people. The spirit in the second dream actually leads the dreamer to the church-yard, where he is to mark a particular grave by defecating on it. A part of this situation is very easy to understand. The sleeper knows that the bed is not the proper place for satisfying his need; hence in the dream he causes himself to be led away from it and procures a person who shows his hidden urge the right way to another place where he is permitted to satisfy his need, indeed is required by the circumstances to do so. The spirit in the second dream actually makes use of a candle when leading him, as a servant would do if he was conducting a stranger to the lavatory at night when it was dark. But why are these representatives of the demand for a change of scene, which the lazy sleeper wants to avoid at all costs, such uncanny individuals as ghosts and spirits of dead people? Why does the spirit in the second dream lead the way to a churchyard as if to desecrate a grave? After all, these elements seem to have nothing to do with the urge to defecate and the symbolization of feces by gold. There is an indication in them of an anxiety which could perhaps be traced back to an effort to suppress the achievement of satisfaction in bed; but that anxiety would not explain

[42]

the specific nature of the dream content—its reference to death. We will refrain from making an interpretation at this point and will stress further, as being in need of explanation, the fact that in both these situations, where two men are sleeping together, the uncanny element of the ghostly guide is associated with a woman. The spirit in the first dream is early on revealed as a beautiful woman who feels she is now released, and the spirit in the second dream leads the way to the grave of a girl, on which the distinguishing mark is to be placed.

Let us turn for further enlightenment to some other defecation dreams of this kind, in which the bedfellows are no longer two men but a man and a woman, a married couple. The satisfying action accomplished in sleep as a result of the dream seems here particularly repellent, but perhaps for that very reason conceals a special meaning.

First, however, we will introduce a dream (on account of its connection in content with those that follow) which does not, strictly speaking, fit in with the plan we have just put forward. It is incomplete, inasmuch as the element of the dreamer's dirtying his bedfellow, his wife, is absent. On the other hand, the connection between the urge to defecate and the fear of death is extremely plain. The peasant, who is described as married, dreams that he is struck by lightning and that his soul flies up to Heaven. Up there he begs to be allowed to return once more to the earth in order to see his wife and children, obtains permission to transform himself into a spider and to let himself down on the thread spun by himself. The thread is too short and the effort to express still more thread out of his body results in defecation.

DREAM AND REALITY[9]

A peasant lay in bed and had a dream. He saw himself in the field with his oxen, ploughing. Then suddenly down came a flash of lightning and struck him dead. Then he felt quite clearly his soul floating upwards until at last it reached Heaven. Peter stood by the entrance gates and was going to send the peasant in without more ado. But he begged to be allowed down to earth once more, so that he could at least take leave of his wife and his children. But Peter said that would not do, and once a man was in Heaven he was not allowed to return to the world. At this the peasant wept and begged pitifully, until at last Peter gave way. Now there was only one possible way for the peasant to see his family again and that was for Peter to change him into an animal and send him down. So the peasant was turned into a spider and spun a long thread on which he let him-

---

[9] Dr. von Waldheim, "Skatologische Erzählungen aus Preussisch-Schlesien [Scatologic Tales from Prussian Silesia]," *Anthropophyteia, 6,* 431, No. 9.

self down. When he had arrived just over his homestead, at about the level of the chimneys, and could already see his children playing in the meadow, he noticed to his horror that he could not spin any further. Naturally his fear was great, for of course he wanted to get right down to the earth. So he squeezed and he squeezed to make the thread longer. He squeezed with all his might and main—there was a loud noise—and the peasant awoke. Something very human had happened to him while he slept.

Here we encounter spun thread as a new symbol for evacuated feces, although psychoanalysis furnishes us with no counterpart to this symbolization but on the contrary attributes another symbolic meaning to thread. This contradiction will be settled later on. [P. 49.]

The next dream, richly elaborated and pungently told, might be described as a "sociable" one; it ends with the wife's being dirtied. Its points of agreement with the previous dream are, however, quite striking. The peasant is, it is true, not dead, but he finds himself in heaven, wants to return to the earth and experiences the same difficulty over "spinning" a sufficiently long thread to let himself down on. However, he does not make this thread for himself as a spider out of his own body, but in a less fantastic way out of everything that he can fasten together, and as the thread is still not long enough, the little angels actually advise him to shit and to lengthen the rope with the turds.

THE PEASANT'S ASSUMPTION TO HEAVEN[10]

A peasant had the following dream. He had heard that wheat in Heaven was standing at a high price. So he thought he would like to take his wheat there. He loaded his cart, harnessed the horse and set out. He journeyed a long way till he saw the road to Heaven and followed it. Thus he came to the gates of Heaven, and look! they stood open. He charged straight forward so as to drive right inside, but he had scarcely headed the cart toward them when— crash! the gates banged shut. Then he began to beg: "Let me in, please be kind!" But the angels did not let him in and said he had come late. Then he saw that there was no business to be done here; there was just nothing for him, and so he turned round. But look! the road he had traveled on had vanished. What was he to do? He addressed himself to the angels again. "Little dears, please be kind and take me back to the earth, if it's possible! give me a road so that I can get home with my horse and cart!" But the angels said: "No, child of man, your horse and cart stay here and you can go down how you please." "But how shall I let myself down then, I haven't any rope?" "Just look for something to let yourself down with." So he took the reins, the bridle and the bit, fastened them all together and began to let himself down. He

---

[10] Tarasevsky, *op. cit.,* 196 [No. 233].

[46]

crawled and he crawled and he looked down—it was still a long way to the earth. He crawled back again and lengthened the rope he had joined together by adding the girth and the traces. Then he began to climb down again and it still did not reach the earth. So he fastened on the shafts and the body of the cart. It was still too short. What was he to do next? He racked his brains and then he thought: "Ah, I'll lengthen it with my coat and my breeches and my shirt and then with my belt." And that is what he did, joined everything together and climbed on. When he had reached the end of the belt it was still a long way to the earth. Then he did not know what to do; he had nothing more to fasten on and it was dangerous to jump down: he might break his neck. He begged the angels again: "Be kind, take me down to the earth!" The angels said: "Shit, and the muck will make a rope." So he shat and he shat almost half an hour until he had nothing left to shit with. It made a long rope and he climbed down it. He climbed and he climbed and reached the end of the rope, but it was still a long way to the earth. Then he began once more to beg the angels to take him down to the earth. But the angels said: "Now, child of man, piss and it will make a silken thread." The peasant pissed and he pissed, on and on, till he could do no more. He saw that it really had turned into a silken thread and he climbed on. He climbed and he climbed and he reached the end of it, and look, it did not reach to the earth, it still needed one and a half or two fathoms. He begged the angels again to take him down. But the angels said: "No, brother, there is no help for you

now; just jump down!" The peasant dangled unde-
cided; he could not find the courage to jump down.
But then he saw that there was no other way out left
to him, and bump! instead of jumping down from
Heaven he came flying down from the stove and only
came to his senses in the middle of the room. Then
he woke up and shouted: "Wife, wife, where are
you?" His wife woke up, she heard the din and said:
"The Devil take you, have you gone mad?" She felt
round about her and saw the mess: her husband had
shat and pissed all over her. She began to rate and
to scold him roundly. The peasant said: "What are
you screaming about? There's vexation enough any-
way. The horse is lost, stayed behind in Heaven, and
I was almost done for. God be thanked that I am
alive at least!" "What rubbish you're talking. You've
had much too much to drink. The horse is in the
stable and you were on the stove, and dirtied me all
over and then jumped down." Then the man collected himself. Only then did it dawn on him that he
had merely dreamt it all; and then he told his wife the
dream, how he had journeyed up to Heaven and how
from there he came down to the earth again.

At this point, however, psychoanalysis forces on
our attention an interpretation which changes our
whole view of this class of dreams. Extensible ob-
jects, so the experience of interpreting dreams tells
us, are ordinarily symbols of erection.[11] In both

---

[11] [*Marginal Note by* Oppenheim:] In a story which comes
from Picardy, pushing a ring down on a finger serves as a

these anecdotes of dreams the emphasis lies on the element of the thread's refusing to get long enough, and the anxiety in the dream is also attached to this same element. Thread, moreover, like all things analogous to it (cord, rope, twine, etc.), is a symbol of semen.[12] The peasant, then, is striving to produce an erection and only when this is unsuccessful does he resort to defecation. All at once a sexual need comes to view in these dreams behind the excremental one.

This sexual need is, however, much better adapted to explain the remaining constituents of the dream's content. We are bound to admit, if we are ready to assume that these fictitious dreams are essentially correctly constructed, that the dream action with which they end must have a meaning and must be one intended by the latent thoughts of the dreamer. If the dreamer defecates over his wife at the end of it, then the whole dream must have this as its aim and provide the reason for this outcome. It can signify nothing else but an insult to the wife, or strictly speaking, a rejection of her. It is then easy to establish a connec-

---

symbolic way of depicting an erection. The lower the ring goes, the longer the penis becomes—the analogy naturally has a magical force. *(Kryptadia, 1,* No. 32.) [That is, it is an instance of what Frazer calls "imitative magic."]

[12] Cf. Stekel, *Die Sprache des Traumes,* Wiesbaden, 1911.

tion between this and the deeper significance of the anxiety expressed in the dream.

The situation from which this last dream grows can be construed according to these suggestions as follows. The sleeper is overcome by a strong erotic need which is indicated in fairly clear symbols at the beginning of the dream. (He had heard that wheat—probably equivalent to semen—was standing at a high price. He charged forward in order to drive with his horse and cart—genital symbols —through the open gates of Heaven.) But this libidinal impulse probably applies to an unattainable object. The gates close, he gives up his intention and wants to return to the earth. But his wife, who lies by him, does not attract him; he exerts himself in vain to get an erection for her. The wish to discard her in order to replace her by another and better woman is in the infantile sense a death wish. When someone cherishes such wishes in his unconscious against a person who is nevertheless really loved, they are transformed for him into fear of death, fear for his own life. Hence the presence in these dreams of the state of being dead, the assumption to Heaven, the hypocritical longing to see wife and children again. But the disappointed sexual libido finds release along the path of regression in the excremental wishful impulse, which abuses and soils the unserviceable sexual object.

If this particular dream makes an interpretation of this kind plausible, then, in view of the peculiarities of the material which the dream contains, we can only succeed in proving the interpretation by applying the same one to a whole succession of dreams with an allied content. With this aim in view, let us turn back to the dreams mentioned earlier, where we find the situation of a sleeper who has a man as his bedfellow. The connection in which the woman appears in these dreams now acquires an added significance in retrospect. The sleeper, overcome by a libidinal impulse, rejects the man; he wishes him far away and a woman in his place. A death wish directed against the dreamer's unwanted male bedfellow is naturally not so severely punished by the moral censorship as one directed against his wife, but the reaction is sufficiently far-reaching to turn the wish against himself or against the female object he desires. The dreamer himself is carried off by death; not the man, but the woman the dreamer longs for, is dead. In the end, however, the rejection of the male sexual object finds an outlet in defiling him, and this is felt and avenged by the other as an affront.

Our interpretation thus fits this group of dreams. If we now turn back to the dreams accompanied by defilement of the woman, we shall be prepared to find that elements missing or only hinted at in the dream we have taken as the type are expressed unmistakably in other similar dreams.

In the following defecation dream the dirtying of the woman is not emphasized, but we are told quite clearly, as far as can be in the realm of symbolism, that the libidinal impulse is directed toward another woman. The dreamer does not want to dirty his own field, but intends to defecate on his neighbor's land.

MUTTONHEAD![13]

A peasant dreamt that he was at work in his clover field. He was overtaken by an urgent need and, since he did not want to foul his own clover, he hurried off to the tree standing in his neighbor's field, pulled down his breeches and slapped down a pat of number two onto the ground. At last, when he had happily come to an end, he wanted to clean himself and began to tear up grass with a will. But what was that? Our little peasant woke up from his sleep with a jerk, and clutched at his painfully smarting cheek which someone had just slapped. "You deaf old muttonhead!"—the peasant, coming to himself, heard his wife in bed beside him scolding, "So you'd go on pulling the hair right off my body would you!"

---

[13] F. Wernert, "Deutsche Bauernerzählungen gesammelt im Ober- und Unterelsass [German Peasant Tales, Collected in Upper and Lower Alsace]," *Anthropophyteia, 4,* 138, No. 173.

Tearing out hair (grass), which here takes the place of defiling,[14] is found mentioned alongside it in the next dream. Psychoanalytic experience shows that it originates from the group of symbols concerning masturbation *(ausreissen, abreissen* [to pull out, to pull off]).[15]

The dreamer's death wish directed against his wife would seem to be what most requires confirming in our interpretation. But in the dream which follows next, the dreamer actually buries his wife (hypocritically designated as a treasure) by digging the vessel which contains the gold into the earth and, as is familiar to us in dreams about treasure, planting a heap of feces on the top to mark the place. During the digging he is working his hands in his wife's vagina.[16]

THE DREAM OF THE TREASURE[17]

Once upon a time a peasant had a terrible dream. It seemed to him just like it was wartime and the whole district was being plundered by the enemy

---

[14] [At this point there is a question mark by Oppenheim in the margin of the manuscript.]

[15] [Cf. a footnote in *The Interpretation of Dreams, Standard Ed.,* 5, 348, *n.2.* These are German slang terms for "to masturbate." Compare the English equivalent "to toss oneself off."]

[16] [*Marginal Note by* Oppenheim:] Significance?

[17] A. Riedl, "Schwänke und Schnurren niederösterreichischer Landleute [Comic and Curious Anecdotes from Lower-Austrian Country People]," *Anthropophyteia,* 5, 140, No. 19.

soldiers. But he had a treasure that he was so scared about that he didn't rightly know what to do with it and where he should really hide it. At last he thought he would bury it in his garden, where he knew of a proper fine place. Now he dreams on further how he goes right out and comes to the place where he wants to dig up the earth so he can put the big pot in the hole. But when he looks for a tool to dig with he finds nix roundabout, and at last he has to take his hands to it. So he makes the hole with his bare hands, puts the crock with the money into it and covers the whole lot over again with earth. Now he wants to go, but he stops a while standing there and thinks to himself: "But when the soldiers have gone away again, how'll I find my treasure then if I don't put a sign there?" And straight away he begins to hunt about; he hunts up and down and to and fro, wherever he can. No, in the end he finds nix nowhere that would show him again straight away where he has buried his money. But just then he feels a need. "Ah," he says to himself, "now that'll be fine, I can shit on it." So of course he pulls his breeches down right away and does a fine heap on the place where he has put the crock in. Then he sees nearby a bit of grass and is going to pull it out, so he can wipe himself with it. But that moment he gets such a fine clout that for a second he is quite silly and looks round all dazed. And straight after he hears his wife, who is quite beside herself with rage, yelling at him: "You cheeky bastard, you good-for-nothing! D'you think I've got to put up with everything from you? First you mess about with both hands in my cunt, then you shit on it and now you even want to pull all the hair off of it!"

With this example of a dream we have returned to the treasure dreams from which we started out, and we observe that those defecation dreams which are concerned with treasure contain little or no fear of death, whereas the others, in which the relation to death is expressed directly (dreams of an assumption to Heaven), disregard treasure and motivate the defecation in other ways. It is almost as though the hypocritical transformation of the wife into a treasure had obviated punishment for the death wish.[18]

A death wish directed against the woman is most clearly admitted to in another dream of an assumption to Heaven, which, however, ends not in defecating on the woman's body but in sexual activity involving her genitals, as already happened in the previous dream. The dreamer actually shortens his wife's life in order to lengthen his own, by putting oil from her lamp of life into his own. As a kind of compensation for this undisguised hostility there appears at the end of the dream something like an attempt at a caress.

---

[18] [*Marginal Note by* Oppenheim] What about the treasure in the dreams of one of two male bedfellows [p. 40]?

The Light of Life[19]

Saint Peter appeared to a man when he was fast asleep and led him away to Paradise. The man agreed to go with all his heart and went with Saint Peter. They wandered about in Paradise for a long time and came to a copse, which was large and spacious but kept in beautiful order, and where hanging lamps were burning on every tree. The man asked Saint Peter what this could mean. Saint Peter answered that they were hanging lamps which only burned as long as a man lived. But as soon as the oil vanished and the lamp went out, the man had to die at once too. This interested the man very much and he asked Saint Peter if he would lead him to his own hanging lamp. Saint Peter granted his request and led him to his wife's lamp, and just by it was the man's own lamp. The man saw that his wife's lamp still had a lot of oil in it, but there was very little in his own and this made him very sorry because he would have to die soon, and he asked Saint Peter if he would pour a little more oil into his lamp. Saint Peter said that God put the oil in at the moment when a man was born and determined for each the length of his life. This made the man very downcast and he wept and wailed beside his lamp. Saint Peter said to him: "You stay there, but I must go on—I have more to do." The man rejoiced at this and hardly was Saint Peter out of sight when he began to dip his finger in his wife's

<hr>

[19] Narrated by a Secondary School teacher in Belgrade, based on a version told by a peasant woman from the region of Kragujevac. *Anthropophyteia, 4,* 255, No. 10.

hanging lamp and to drip the oil into his own. He did this several times and when Saint Peter approached he started up terrified, and awoke from his dream, and saw that he had been dipping his finger in his wife's cunt and then dribbling it into his mouth and licking his finger.

Note.—According to a version told by a journeyman in Sarajevo, the man awoke after getting a box on the ears from his wife, whom he had awakened by fumbling around in her pudenda. Here Saint Peter is missing and instead of hanging lamps there are glasses with oil burning in them. According to a third version, which I heard from a student in Mostar, a venerable greybeard shows the man various candles. His own is very thin, his wife's enormously thick. In order to lengthen his life, the man then begins with burning zeal to lick the thick candle. But then he gets a tremendous clout. "I knew that you were an ox, but I honestly didn't know that you were a swine as well," his wife said to him, for he was licking her cunt in his sleep.

The story is extraordinarily widespread in Europe.[20]

This is the moment to recall the "bad dream" of the woman who ended by pulling at her husband's organ as if she wanted to tear it out [p. 31]. The interpretation which we found reason to make in that instance agrees completely with the

---

[20] [*Marginal Note by* Oppenheim:] Cf. a very similar story from the Ukraine, *Kryptadia*, 5, 15.

interpretation of the defecation dreams dreamt by men which is expounded here. In the dream of the unsatisfied wife, she, as well, shamelessly gets rid of her husband (and the child) as obstacles in the way of satisfaction.

Another defecation dream, about whose interpretation we cannot perhaps be completely certain, suggests, however, that we should concede that there are certain differences in the purpose of these dreams, and throws new light on dreams like the ones we have just mentioned and on some that are still to follow, in which the dream action consists in a manipulation of the woman's genitals.

"FROM FRIGHT"[21]

The Pasha passed the night with the Bey. When the next day came, the Bey[22] lay on in bed and did not want to get up. The Bey asked the Pasha: "What did you dream?" "I dreamt that on the minaret there was another minaret." "Could that really be?" wondered the Bey. "And what else did you dream?" "I dreamt," he said, "that on the minaret there stood a copper jug, and there was water in the jug. The wind blew and the copper jug rocked. Now what would you have done if you had dreamt that?" "I should have

---

[21] F. S. Krauss, "Südslavische Volksüberlieferungen, die sich auf den Geschlechtsverkehr beziehen [Southern Slav Folk Traditions Concerning Sexual Intercourse]," *Anthropophyteia*, 5, 293, No. 697.

pissed myself and shat myself as well, from fright."
"And, you see, I only pissed myself."

This dream calls for a symbolic interpretation, because its manifest content is quite incomprehensible whereas the symbols are unmistakably clear. Why should the dreamer really feel frightened at the sight of a water jug rocking on the tip of a minaret? But a minaret is excellently suited to be a symbol for the penis, and the rhythmically moving water vessel seems a good symbol of the female genitals in the act of copulation. The Pasha, then, has had a copulation dream, and if his host suggests defecation in connection with it this makes it likely that the interpretation is to be sought in the circumstance that both of them are old and impotent men, in whom old age has occasioned the same proverbial replacement of sexual by excremental pleasure which, as we have seen, came about in the other dreams owing to the lack of an appropriate sexual object. For a man who can no longer copulate, so say the common people with their crude love of truth, there still remains the pleasure of shitting; we can say of such a man there is a recurrence of anal erotism, which was there before genital erotism and was

22 [This should probably read "the Pasha," though it appears as "the Bey" in both the German and the Slav versions in *Anthropophyteia*.]

repressed and replaced by this later impulse. Defecation dreams can thus also be impotence dreams.

The difference between the interpretations is not so pronounced as might appear at first sight. The defecation dreams too, in which the victim is a woman, deal with impotence—relative impotence, at least, toward the particular person who no longer has any attraction for the dreamer. A defecation dream thus becomes the dream of a man who can no longer satisfy a woman, as well as of a man whom a woman no longer satisfies.

The same interpretation (as an impotence dream) can also be applied to a dream in the *Facetiae* of Poggio, which manifestly, it is true, poses as the dream of a jealous man—that is, in fact, of a man who does not think he can satisfy his wife.

THE RING OF FIDELITY[23]

Franciscus Philelphus was jealous of his wife and became tormented by the greatest fear that she had to do with another man, and day and night he lay on the watch. Since what occupies us in waking is wont to return to us in dreams, there appeared to him during his sleep a demon, who said to him that if he would act according to his bidding his wife would always remain faithful to him. Franciscus said to him in the

[23] Poggio [Bracciolini], *Facetiae*, No. 133.

dream that he would be very indebted to him and promised him a reward.

"Take this ring," replied the demon, "and wear it on your finger with care. As long as you wear it, your wife cannot lie with any other man without your knowledge."

As he awoke, excited with joy, he felt that he was pushing his finger into the vulva of his wife.

The jealous have no better expedient; in this way their wives can never let themselves be taken by another man without the knowledge of their husbands.

This anecdote of Poggio is considered to be the source of[24] a tale by Rabelais, which, in other respects very similar, is clearer inasmuch as it actually describes the husband bringing home a young wife in his old age, who then gives him grounds for jealous fears.[25]

Hans Carvel was a learned, experienced, industrious man, a man of honor, of good understanding and judgment, benevolent, charitable to the poor and a cheerful philosopher. Withal a good companion, who was fond of a jest, somewhat corpulent and unsteady, but otherwise well set up in every way. In his old age he married the daughter of Concordat the bailiff, a young, comely, good, gay, lively and pleasing woman,

---

24 [The manuscript reads "to be derived from." But this must be a slip, since Poggio's *Facetiae* were in print by about 1470, some twenty-five years before Rabelais was born.]

25 Rabelais, *Pantagruel,* Chapter 28 of *Le Tiers Livre.*

merely perchance a little too friendly toward the gentlemen neighbors and manservants. So it befell that
in the course of some weeks he became as jealous as
a tiger and was suspicious that she might be getting
her buttocks drummed upon elsewhere. To guard
against this, he related to her a whole stock of pleasing
histories of the punishments for adultery, often read
to her aloud lovely legends of virtuous women,
preached her the gospel of chastity, wrote her a small
volume of songs of praise to matrimonial fidelity, in-
veighed in sharp and caustic words against the wan-
tonness of undisciplined wives, and in addition to all
bestowed on her a magnificent necklace set round
with oriental sapphires.

But regardless of this, he saw her going about with
the neighbors in such a friendly and sociable fashion
that his jealousy mounted yet higher. One night at
that time, as he was lying with her in bed, in the midst
of these painful thoughts, he dreamt he spoke with
the Fiend Incarnate and bewailed his grief to him.
But the Devil comforted him, put a ring on his finger
and said: "Take this ring; as long as you carry it on
your finger no other man can have carnal knowledge
of your wife without your knowledge and against
your will." "A thousand thanks, Sir Devil," said Hans
Carvel, "I will deny Mahomet before ever I take this
ring from my finger." The Devil disappeared. But
Hans Carvel awoke with a joyful heart and found
that he had his finger in his wife's what-d'you-call-it.

I forgot to relate how the young woman, when she
felt this, jerked her buttocks backwards as if to say:
"Stop! No, No! That's not what ought to be put

in there!"—which made Hans Carvel imagine that someone wanted to pull off his ring.

Is that not an infallible measure? Believe me! act after this example and take care at all times to have your wife's ring on your finger![26]

The Devil, who appears here as counselor, as he does in the treasure dreams, gives us a clue to something of the dreamer's latent thoughts. Originally, at least, he was supposed to "take" the unfaithful wife who is hard to keep a watch on.[27] He then shows in the manifest dream an infallible means of keeping her permanently. In this too we recognize an analogy with the wish to get rid of someone (death wish) in the defecation dreams.

We will conclude this small collection of dreams by adding a lottery dream, whose connection with the others is rather slight, but which serves to confirm the suggestion which we put forward

---

[26] [*Footnote by* Freud:] Goethe is concerned with this symbolism of the ring and the finger in a Venetian Epigram (*Paralipomena,* No. 65, Sophienausgabe, Abt. II, Bd. 5, 381).
Costly rings I possess! Excellent stones, engraved
In lofty style and conception, held by the purest of gold.
Dearly men pay for these rings, adorned with fiery stones,
Oft have you seen them sparkle over the gaming-table.
But one little ring I know, whose virtue is not the same,
Which Hans Carvel once possessed, sadly, when he was old.
Foolish he pushed in the ring the smallest of all his ten fingers,
The eleventh, the biggest, alone is worthy and fit to be there.
[27] [Here there is a question mark by Oppenheim in the margin.]

earlier [p. 35] that a lottery symbolizes a marriage contract.

IT'S NO USE CRYING OVER SPILT MILK![28]

A merchant had a strange dream. He dreamt that he saw a woman's arse with everything that belonged to it. On one half was a figure 1 and on the other a 3. Before this, the merchant had had the idea of buying a lottery ticket. It seemed to him that this picture in his dream was a lucky omen. Without waiting till the ninth hour, he ran to the bank first thing in the morning, in order to buy his ticket. He arrived there and without pausing to think he demanded ticket Number Thirteen, the same figures that he had seen in his dream. After he had bought his ticket, not a day passed on which he did not look in all the newspapers to see if his number had won. After a week, or at the most after ten days, the list of the draw came out. When he looked through, he saw that his number had not been drawn but the number 103, Series 8, and that number had won 200,000 roubles. The merchant nearly tore his hair out. "I must have made a mistake! there is something wrong!" He was beside himself, he was almost inconsolable and could not conceive what his having had such a dream could mean. Then he resolved to discuss the matter with his friend to see if he could not account for his misfortune. He met his friend and told him everything in minute detail. Then his friend said: "Oh you simpleton! Didn't you see the nought between the num-

[28] Tarasevsky, *op. cit.*, 40 [No. 63].

ber 1 and the 3 on the arse?" "A-a-ah, the Devil take it, it never occurred to me that the arse had a nought." "But it was there plain and clear, only you didn't work out the lottery number right. And the number 8 belonging to the series—the cunt shows you that—it's like a number 8."—It's no use crying over spilt milk!

Our intention in putting together this short paper was twofold. On the one hand, we wanted to suggest that one should not be deterred by the often repulsively dirty and indecent nature of this popular material from seeking in it valuable confirmation of psychoanalytic views. Thus on this occasion we have been able to establish the fact that folklore interprets dream symbols in the same way as psychoanalysis, and that, contrary to loudly proclaimed popular opinion, it derives a group of dreams from needs and wishes which have become immediate. On the other hand, we should like to express the view that it is doing the common people an injustice to assume that they employ this form of entertainment merely to satisfy the coarsest desires. It seems rather that behind these ugly façades are concealed mental reactions to impressions of life which are to be taken seriously, which even strike a sad note—reactions to which common people are ready to surrender, but only if they are accompanied by a yield of coarse pleasure.

PART II

TRÄUME IM FOLKLORE

The original German text

von

SIGM. FREUD

und

PROF. ERNST OPPENHEIM

TRÄUME
IM FOLKLORE

"CELSI PRAETEREUNT AUSTERA POEMATA RAMNES."
PERSIUS, *Satirae*

Der eine von uns (O.) hat bei seinen Folklore-
studien an den dort erzälten* Träumen zwei
Beobachtungen gemacht, die ihm der Mitteilung
wert erschienen sind. Erstens dass die in diesen
Träumen angewendete Symbolik sich vollkommen
mit der von den Psychoanalytikern angenomme-
nen deckt, und zweitens, dass eine Anzal dieser
Träume vom Volke so gefasst wird, wie sie auch
die Psychoanalyse deuten würde, nämlich nicht
als Hinweise auf eine zu enthüllende Zukunft,
sondern als Wunscherfüllungen, Befriedigungen
von Bedürfnissen, die sich während des Schlaf-
zustandes zeigen. Gewisse Eingenheiten dieser
durchwegs indezenten als Schwänke erzälten
Träume haben es dann dem anderen von uns
(Fr.) nahe gelegt, eine Deutung derselben zu ver-
suchen, welche sie doch als ernsthafter und beach-
tenswerter erscheinen lässt.

---

* [Freud's original spelling has been preserved throughout.]

[69]

I.

PENIS-SYMBOLIK IN FOLKLORE-TRÄUMEN.

Der Traum den wir voranstellen, obwol er keine symbolische Darstellung enthält, klingt fast wie ein Hohn auf die prophetische und ein Plaidoyer für die psychologische Traumdeutung.

PROPHETISCHE UND PSYCHOLOGISCHE TRAUMDEUTUNG.

PENISSYMBOLE 1

Anthrop. VII.S.450
Südslavische Volksüberlieferungen, die sich auf den Geschlechtsverkehr beziehen, gesammelt und erläutert v. Fr. S. Krauss

No. 820: *Eine Traumdeutung.*

Ein Mädchen erhob sich von ihrer Bettstatt und erzählte der Mutter, wie ihr ein gar wunderbarer Traum geträumt.

Nun, was hat die da geträumt? fragte sie die Mutter.

Wie soll ich es dir nur sagen, ich weiss selber nicht wie, so etwas langes, rotes und abgestumpftes.

Das lange bedeutet einen Weg, sagte die Mutter nachsinnend, einen langen Weg, das rote bedeutet Freude, doch weiss ich nicht, was ihm das abgestumpfte bedeuten mag.

Des Mädchens Vater, der sich inzwischen ankleidete

und alles mit anhörte, was Mutter und Tochter daherredeten, murmelte da mehr in sich hinein: "Das gleicht ja einigermassen meinem Prächtigen." Vgl. dazu Anthrop. I. S. 4. No. 5

Das judendeutsche Sprichwort: Die Gans träumt vom Kukuruz und die Kalle (Braut) vom Wonz (Zumpt).

Es ist sehr viel bequemer die Traumsymbolik im Folklore als in den wirklichen Träumen zu studieren. Der Traum ist genötigt zu verbergen und liefert seine Geheimnisse nur der Deutung aus; diese Schwänke aber, die sich als Träume verkleiden, wollen mittheilen, zur Lust dessen, der sie vorbringt wie dessen, der sie anhört, und setzen deshalb die Deutung ungescheut zum Symbol hinzu. Sie freuen sich der Bloslegung der verhüllenden Symbole.

Im nachstehenden Vierzeiler erscheint der Penis als Szepter:

Penissymbole 3

2. Niederösterreich. Schnadahüpfeln
   Anthr. V 152
S. 151 Niederösterreichische Schnadahüpfeln.
   Gesam. v. Dr. Herm. Rollett.

No. 2: Heut Nacht hat ma tramt i wa König im Land,
   Und wie i bin munter wurn hab i in Schwaf in
   da Hand.

[71]

Man vergleiche mit diesem "Traum" die folgenden Beispiele in denen die naemliche Symbolik ausserhalb des Traumes gebraucht wird.

Krypt. IV S. 111 N. 160
(aus den österr. Alpen)

Herzig schöns Deandl
I hab di so gern
Gib dir n Zepter ind Hand
Kannst Königin wern.

Aus Gaming Nied. Österr.
Anthrop. III 190 N. 85, 4

Napoleon Bonaparte sprach
Einst zu seinem Sohne
So lang der Schwanz das Zepter is
Bleibt die Fut die Krone

Der künstlerischen Phantasie beliebt eine andersartige Variation dieser symbolischen Verherrlichung des Genitales. Auf einem grossartigen Blatte von *Felicien Rops** das die Überschrift führt: "Tout est grand chez les rois" sieht man eine nackte Königsgestalt mit den Zügen des Roi Soleil, dessen riesenhafter, bis zur Höhe der Hände erhobener Penis selbst eine Krone trägt. Die rechte Hand balanciert ein Szepter, während die linke einen grossen Reichsapfel umfasst der durch eine mittlere Furche eine unverkennbare Ähnlich-

---

* das erotische Werk des *Felicien Rops*. Zweiundvierzig Radierungen. Privatdruck 1905.

keit mit einem anderen erotisch begehrten Kör-
perteil gewinnt. Der Zeigefinger der linken Hand
ist in diese Spalte eingeschlagen (Blatt 20).

[Randbemerkung, E.O.]
   Wie bei Rops der Apfel ist auf einem röm. Relief
des Amphitheaters von Nimes das Ei durch eine
entsprechende Einkerbung zum Symbol des weibl.
Geschlechtsteiles umgestaltet. Auch hier fehlt das
männliche Komplement nicht. Es erscheint als ein
zum Vogel wunderlich herausstaffierter Phallus, der
auf 4 Eiern der geschilderten Art sitzt, man könnte
fast (stenographisch: sagen) brütet.
(Kraus, ... S 204 Abb. N. 191)

In dem nun mitzutheilenden schlesischen Volks-
lied wird ein Traum nur fingiert, um einen anderen Hergang zu decken. Der Penis erscheint
hier als *Wurm* (dicker Regenwurm), der in das
Mädchen hineingekrochen ist, und zur richtigen
Zeit als *Würmchen* (Kind) wieder herauskriecht.

Anthrop. VII. S. 369

Penissymbole 2 *(Wurm)*

Schlesische Volkslieder aufgezeichnet von
Dr. v. Waldheim

Lied vom Regenwurm

Susanna lag im feuchten Grase
Und träumte schlummernd von dem Lieb,
Ein Lächeln spielte um Ihre Nase,
Sie dachte an den Herzensdieb.

Da plötzlich ward, o Traum, o banger,
Aus ihrem Liebsten hold und fein
Ein dicker Regenwurm, ein langer,
Der kroch ihr in den Bauch hinein.

Voll Schreck erwacht das junge Mädchen
Und eilte weinend hin zum Städtchen,
Erzählte jammernd gross und klein;
"Ein Regenwurm kroch in mich 'nein."

Die Mutter hörte diesen Jammer
Und hat gezetert und geflucht,
Sie zog das Mädchen in die Kammer
Und hat es gründlichst untersucht.

Sie forschte nach dem Regenwurme,
Doch leider ohne Resultat,
Drum eilte sie davon im Sturme
Und hat 'ne weise Frau gefragt.

Die legte dem Mädchen gar schlau die Karten
Und sprach darauf: "Wir müssen warten.
Herzbube hab' ich umsonst befragt,
Will sehen, was der König sagt.—

Rotkönig zeigte klar und deutlich,
Der Wurm kroch wirklich in die Maid,
Doch ist's zum Eingriff noch zu zeitlich,
Denn jedes Ding braucht seine Zeit."

Susanna hört die trübe Kunde
Und schloss sich traurig ein zuhaus.
Da endlich naht die bange Stunde
Und glücklich kriecht das Würmchen aus.

Drum, Mädchen, nehmt euch bei der Nase
Und schlummert träumend nicht im Grase,
Sonst kriecht euch auch zur Angst und Pein
So 'n dicker Regenwurm hinein.—

Vgl.dazu S/359 und die südslav.Fassungen bei Krauss,
Die Zeugung in Sitte, Brauch und Glauben d. Südslaven, Kryptadia VI. S.259-269 u. S.375 f. Anmerkung des Herausgebers.

Die gleiche Symbolisirung des Penis als *Wurm*
ist aus zalreichen zotigen Witzen bekannt.*

Der nun folgende Traum symbolisirt den Penis
als *Dolch,* indem er die träumende Frau an einem
Dolch ziehen lässt, um sich zu erstechen, während
sie vom Manne geweckt und gemahnt wird, ihm
nicht das Glied auszureissen.

S. 289   *Ein böser Traum.*

Es träumte einem Frauenzimmer, es wäre mit
ihnen so weit gekommen, dass sie vor dem Feiertag
nichts zu essen hatten und auch nichts kaufen konnten. Ihr Mann hatte alles Geld vertrunken. Es blieb
nur ein Lotterielos und auch dies sollte man schon
jemandem zum Pfand geben. Dies hielt er noch zurück, denn am zweiten Jänner sollte die Ziehung sein.
Er sagte: "Nun Frau, morgen ist die Ziehung, mag das
Los noch eine zeitlang bleiben. Wenn wir nicht
gewinnen, dann müssen wir das Los verkaufen oder
versetzen."—"Nun zum Teufel mit ihm, zahlst du

---

* [E. O.] (Anmerk.) (... 5)

nur die Fürchtelei und hast einen Vorteil dabei, wie vom Bock die Milch." So war der Morgen angebrochen. Sieh, da kam der Zeitungsausträger. Er hielt ihn an, nahm eine Nummer und begann die Liste durchzusehen. Er lies die Augen über die Ziffern gleiten, alle Kolonnen schaute er durch, seine Nummer war nicht darunter; er traute seinen Augen nicht, sah nochmals durch und hier traf er schon auf die Nummer seines Loses; und die Nummer des Loses war dieselbe, die Nummer der Serie stimmte aber nicht. Er traute wiederum sich selbst nicht und dachte bei sich: "Das muss ein Irrtum sein. Wart' mal, ich will in die Bank gehen und werde auf jeden Fall Gewissheit erlangen." So ging er hin mit gesenktem Kopf; unterwegs begegnete ihm ein zweiter Zeitungsausträger. Er kaufte noch eine Nummer von einer zweiten Zeitung, durchsah die Liste und hatte sofort die Nummer seines Loses herausgefunden, auch die Serie war dieselbe, die auch sein Los enthielt. Der Gewinn von 5000 Rubeln fiel auf sein Los. Da stürzte er in das Bankhaus, kam dorthin gelaufen und bat, man sollte ihm den Treffer sofort auszahlen. Der Bankier sagte, dass sie nicht eher auszahlen könnten, erst in einer Woche oder auch in zwei. Er begann zu bitten: "Seit so gut, gebt wenigstens einen Tausender her, den Rest kann ich später bekommen." Der Bankier schlug es ihm ab, erteilte ihm aber den Rate, sich an jene Privatperson zu wenden, die ihm das Gewinnlos verschaffte. Nun, was war da zu machen? Da erschien, wie aus dem Boden gewachsen, ein Jüdchen. Er roch den Braten und machte ihm den Vorschlag, ihm sofort das Geld auszuzahlen, aber statt

5000 nur 4000. Der fünfte Tausender sollte ihm zu-
fallen. Er war über dieses Glück erfreut und ent-
schloss sich, dem Juden den Tausender zu schenken,
um nur sofort das Geld zu erhalten. Er nahm vom
Juden das Geld und übergab ihm das Los. Dann ging
er nach Hause; unterwegs trat er in eine Schenke ein,
stürzte ein Gläschen hinab, und von dort ging's direkt
nach Hause; er ging und grinste und summte ein
Liedchen. Das Weib erblickte ihn durch das Fenster
und dachte: Da hat er sicherlich das Los verkauft;
man sieht, dass er fröhlich ist, wahrscheinlich ist er
eingekehrt und hat sich vor Elend angetrunken. Nun
trat er ins Haus ein, legte das Geld auf den Tisch in
der Küche, dann ging er zum Weibe, ihr die fröhliche
Nachricht zu bringen, dass er gewonnen und das Geld
erhalten. Bis sie sich in ihrem Glücke satt umarmt
und abgeküsst erwischte das dreijährige Töchterchen
das Geld und warf es in den Ofen. Nun eilten sie
herbei, das Geld zu zählen, da war es nicht mehr da.
Es brannte das letzte Päckchen. Vor Wut ergriff er das
Mädchen an den Beinen und schleuderte es an den
Ofen. Es gab den Geist auf. Da sah er das Unglück,
Sibirien konnte er nicht entgehen, packte den Re-
volver und—puff, schoss er sich in die Brust, und fort
war sein Geist. Über solch ein Unglück entsetzt,
erwischte sie einen Dolch und wollte sich erstechen.
Sie versuchte ihn aus der Scheide zu ziehen und
konnte es auf keine Weise. Dann hörte sie, wie vom
Himmel eine Stimme: "Genug, lass ab, was machst
Du?" Sie wachte auf und sah, dass sie nicht an einem
Dolch, sondern ihren Mann am Zumpt zog. Und der

sagte ihr: "Genug, lass ab, sonst reisst du mir ihn aus."

Die Darstellung des Penis als Waffe, schneidendes Messer*, Dolch etc. ist uns aus den Angstträumen insbesondere abstinenter Frauen vertraut und liegt auch zalreichen Phobien neurotischer Personen zu Grunde. Die komplizirte Einkleidung des vorstehenden Traumes fordert uns aber zum Versuch heraus, das Verständnis derselben durch psychoanalytische Deutung in Anlehnung an vorher vollzogene Deutungsarbeiten zu klären, wobei wir nicht verkennen, dass wir ein Stück weit über das vom Folklore gebotene hinausgehen und somit an Sicherheit einbüssen.

Da dieser Traum in eine von der Frau als Traumhandlung ausgeführte sexuelle Aggression ausgeht, liegt es nahe, die materielle Notlage des Trauminhaltes zum Ersatz für eine sexuelle Notlage zu nehmen. Nur die äusserste libidinöse Nötigung kann ja eine solche Aggression des Weibes rechtfertigen. Andere Stücke des Trauminhaltes weisen nach einer ganz bestimmten anderen Rich-

---

* [Randbemerkung, E. O.] Das Messer führt gewöhnlich ein "Einbrecher." Welche Art von Einbruch er sinnt zeigt eine sprichwörtl. Redensart: Solingen: nach der Hochzeit wird eingebrochen. (Anth. V 182) natürlich (?) [2 unleserliche stenographische Zeichen] penis als "Brecheisen" (Anth. VII 33 berlinerisch.) [Editor's note: Quotation in Anth. reads: "ein starker Penis."]

tung hin. Die Schuld für diese Notlage wird dem
Manne zugeschrieben (Er hatte alles Geld vertrunken).* Wenn dann der Traum den Mann
und das Kind aus dem Wege räumt und in ge-
schickter Weise dem eigenen Schuldgefül an
diesen Wünschen ausweicht, indem er das Kind
vom Manne töten lässt, worauf sich dieser aus
Reue selbst umbringt, so lässt solcher Inhalt des
Traumes nach vielfachen Analogien auf eine Frau
schliessen, die von ihrem Manne unbefriedigt ist
und in ihrer Phantasie eine andere Ehe ersehnt.
Es ist dabei für die Deutung gleichwertig, ob man
diese Unzufriedenheit der Träumerin als eine
permanente oder nur als Ausdruck ihrer momen-
tanen Bedürftigkeit auffassen will. Die Lotterie,
die im Traume den kurzdauernden Glückstaumel
herbeiführt, könnte man vielleicht als symbolische
Andeutung der Ehe verstehen. Es ist diess Symbol
aus psychoanalytischer Arbeit noch nicht mit
Sicherheit erkannt, aber die Menschen pflegen ja
zu sagen, die Ehe sei ein Glücksspiel, man habe in
der Ehe das grosse Los oder eine Niete gezogen.**
Die Zalen, die durch die Traumarbeit eine unge-

---

* [Randbemerkung, E. O.] vgl. weiter unten unsere Aus-
führungen über Heiratsgut als Bezeichnung des Penis, porte-
monaie für testes u. . . . von reicher Potenz mit Reichtum, von
Golddurst mit libido.
** Ein anderer Lotterietraum in dieser kleinen Sammlung
wird uns in dieser Vermutung bestärken.

heuerliche Vergrösserung erfahren haben* ent-
sprechen dann wol den "Nummern", den ge-
wünschten Wiederholungen des befriedigenden
Aktes. Man wird so aufmerksam gemacht, dass das
Zerren am Glied des Mannes nicht allein die Bedeutung einer libidinösen Provokation hat, sondern auch die Nebenbedeutung einer geringschät-
zigen Kritik, als wollte die Frau das Glied ausreissen,—wie es der Mann richtig auffasst—, weil
es nichts tauge, seine Schuldigkeit nicht thut.

Wir würden nicht bei der Deutung dieses
Traumes verweilt und ihn über die offen vorlie-
gende Symbolik hinaus ausgebeutet haben, wenn
nicht andere Träume, die gleichfalls mit einer
Traumhandlung abschliessen, darthun würden,
dass hier vom Volke eine typische Situation ins
Auge gefasst wird, die einer einheitlichen Zurück-
führung fähig ist. (Vgl. unten).

2. *KOTSYMBOLIK UND ENTSPRECHENDE TRAUMHANDLUNGEN*

Die Psychoanalyse hat uns gelehrt, dass in ur-
anfänglichen Kinderzeiten der Kot eine hoch-
geschätzte Substanz war, an welcher koprophile
Triebe ihre Befriedigung fanden. Mit der durch

---

* Die psychoanalytische Erfahrung zeigt, dass die einer Zal
im Traume angehängten Nullen bei der Deutung weggelassen
werden können.

die Erziehung möglichst beschleunigten Verdrän-
gung dieser Triebe verfiel diese Substanz der
Verachtung und diente nun bewussten Tenden-
zen als Ausdrucksmittel der Geringschätzung und
des Hohnes. Gewisse seelische Arbeitsweisen wie
der Witz verstanden es noch, die verschüttete Lust-
quelle für einen kurzen Moment zugänglich zu
machen, und zeigten so, wie viel von der einstigen
Schätzung des Menschen für seinen Kot im Unbewussten noch erhalten geblieben war. Der
bedeutsamste Rest dieser früheren Wertung war
aber, dass alles Interesse welches das Kind für den
Kot gehabt hatte, sich beim Erwachsenen auf
einen anderen Stoff übertrug, den er im Leben
fast über alles andere hochstellen lernte, auf das
Gold.* Wie alt diese Beziehung zwischen Dreck
und Gold ist, ersieht man aus einer Bemerkung
bei *Jeremias* (babylonisches im alten Testament
1906 p. 96): Das Gold sei nach altorientalischem
Mythus Dreck der Hölle.**

In den Folkloreträumen wird das Gold auf die
eindeutigste Weise als Symbol des Kotes bekannt.
Wenn der Schläfer ein Bedürfnis nach Kotentleerung verspürt, träumt er vom Golde, von einem
Schatz. Die Einkleidung des Traumes, die dazu

---

* Vgl. Charakter und Analerotik. Sammlung kl. Schriften z.
Neurosenlehre. Zweite Folge 1909.
** [Randbemerkung, E. O.] Mexiko.

bestimmt ist, ihn zur Befriedigung des Bedürfnisses im Bette zu verleiten, lässt gewöhnlich den Kothaufen zum Zeichen für die Stelle machen, an welcher der Schatz gefunden ist, d.h: der Traum sagt wie durch endopsychische Wahrnemung direkt, wenn auch in umgekehrter Fassung, das Gold sei ein Zeichen, Symbol, für den Kot.

Ein einfacher solcher Schatz—oder Defaekationstraum ist der in den Facetien des *Poggio* erzälte.

Traumgold

POGGIO: Facetien N.130
(Bd.IV der "Romanischen Meistererzähler" S.103)

Einer erzählt in einer Gesellschaft, dass er im Traume Gold gefunden habe. Darauf gibt ein anderer folgende Geschichte zum besten: (dies wörtlich)

" "Mein Nachbar träumte einmal der Teufel habe ihn auf einen Acker geführt, um Gold zu graben. Er fand aber keines; da sagte der Teufel: "Es ist schon da, du kannst es nur jetzt nicht heben; aber merk dir die Stelle, damit du sie allein wiedererkennen kannst."

Als der andere bat, dass die Stelle durch irgend ein Zeichen kenntlich gemacht würde, meinte der Teufel: Scheiss nur hin, dann wird kein Mensch auf den Gedanken kommen, dass hier Gold verborgen liegt, und du wirst dirs genau merken können. Der Mann tat das auch, wachte dann sofort auf u. fühlte, dass er einen grossen Haufen ins Bett gemacht hatte." "

(Der Schluss im Auszug) Wie er aus dem Hause flüchtet, setzt er sich eine Mütze auf, in die während derselben Nacht eine Katze gemacht hat. Er muss sich Kopf und Haare waschen,

"So wurde ihm sein Traumgold zu Dreck."

Tarasevsky: Geschlechtsleben des ukrainischen Bauernvolkes   S.194   N.122

Im Traume bekommt ein Bauer vom Teufel, dem er eine Kerze geweiht hat, einen Schatz und setzt einen Haufen als Merkmal. [Das Folgende ist in Bleistift, mit zwei stenographischen Zeichen:] Dazu die dabei angegebenen Parallelen   Anth.IV. S.342-345 N.580-581.

Wenn in diesen beiden Träumen der Teufel als Schatzspender und Verführer auftritt, so braucht uns dies nicht zu verwundern, denn der Teufel, selbst ein aus dem Paradies gedrängter Engel, ist doch gewiss nichts anderes als die Personifikation des verdrängten unbewussten Trieblebens.*

Die Motive dieser einfachen Schwankträume scheinen auch durch die zynische Lust am Schmutzigen und durch die boshafte Befriedigung über die Beschämung des Träumers erschöpft. In anderen Schatzträumen aber wird die Einkleidung des Traumes in mannigfacher Weise verwirrt und nimmt verschiedene Bestandteile auf, nach deren

---

* Charakter und Analerotik p. 136.

Herkunft und Bedeutung wir uns fragen dürfen. Denn für ganz willkürlich und bedeutungslos werden wir auch diese Inhalte des Traumes, die die Befriedigung rationalistisch rechtfertigen sollen, nicht ansehen.

In den zwei nächsten Beispielen ereignet sich der Traum nicht einem einsamen Schläfer, sondern einem von zwei Schlafgenossen, die—zwei Männer—ein Bett mit einander teilen. Der Träumer beschmutzt in Folge des Traumes seinen Bettgenossen.

Anthrop.III S.72 (Deutsche Bauernerzählungen gesammelt im Ober- und Unterelsass von F.Wernert) No. 15: *Lebhafter Traum.*

Zwei Handwerkburschen kamen müde in eine Herberge und baten um Nachtquartier. "Ja," sagte der Wirt, "wenn ihr euch nit fürchtet, könnt ihr eine Schlafkammer bekommen, aber da ist es nicht geheuer drinn. Wollt ihr bleiben, bon (gut), dann soll die Herberg, was das Schlafen anlangt, nichts kosten." Gegenseitig fragten sich die Burschen: "Fürchtest du dich?"—"Nein." Gut, so packten sie denn noch einen Liter Wein und gingen alsdann in die angewiesene Kammer.

Kaum lagen sie einige Zeit, da öffnete sich die Türe und eine weisse Gestalt schwebte durch das Gemach. Der eine sagte zum anderen: "Hast du nichts gesehen?"—"Ja."—"Na warum hast du nichts gesagt?" "Warte nur, s' kommt schon wieder durch das Gemach." Richtig, abermals schwebte die Gestalt einher. Rasch sprang der eine Bursche auf, doch noch rascher schwebte das Gespenst zur Türspalte hinaus. Der Bursche nicht faul, reisst die Tür auf und sah die Gestalt, eine schöne Frau, schon auf der halben Treppe gehen. "Was macht Ihr da?" rief der Bursche. Die Gestalt blieb stehen, wendete sich um und sprach "So jetzt bin ich erlöst. Schon lange musst ich wandern. Als Lohn nimm den Schatz, der an der Stelle liegt, wo du eben stehst." Der Bursche war ebensowohl erschrocken als erfreut und um die Stelle zu bezeichnen, hob er sein Hemd auf und pflanzte einen ordentlichen Haufen, in dem er dachte, dieses Zeichen würde keiner verwischen. Doch wie er am glücklichsten ist, fühlt er sich plötzlich gepackt. "Dü Söikaib" (Du Schweinehund) tönt es an seine Ohren, "schiss mer in min Hem" (machst mir in mein Hemd). Bei diesen groben Worten erwachte der glückliche Träumer aus seinem Märchenglück und flog unsanft aus dem Bette.

Siehe dazu Bd. IV, Roman. Meistererzähler No. 130, S.103

[mit Bleistift] Poggio: Facetien: Traumgold

Anthropophyteia B.VI (Skatalogische Erzälungen aus Preuss. Schlesien von Dr. v. *Waldheim*)

S. 346 No. 737: *Er schiss aufs Grab.*

In ein Hotel kehrten zwei Herren ein, assen zu Nacht und tranken und wollten schliesslich schlafen gehen. Sie sagten zum Wirten, er möge ihnen eine Stube anweisen. Da alles besetzt war, überliess ihnen

der Wirt sein Bett, damit sie gemeinsam darin
schlafen, er aber werde sich schon anderswo eine
Schlafstelle ausfindig machen. Die zwei legen sich in
ein Bett nieder. Dem einen erschien im Traum ein
Geist, der eine Kerze anzündete und ihn zum Friedhof hinführte. Das Friedhoftor öffnete sich, der Geist
aber mit der Kerze in der Hand und hinterdrein
dieser Herr schreiten zum Grabe eines Mädchens hin.
Als sie zum Grab hingelangt, verlosch auf einmal
die Kerze. "Was fang ich jetzt an? Wie werde ich
morgen, wenn es Tag worden, erfahren, welches das
Mädchengrab ist?" fragte er im Traume. Es kam ihm
ein rettender Gedanke, er zog die Leinenhosen aus
und beschiss sich aufs Grab. Nachdem er sich beschissen, schlug ihn sein Kamerad, der an seiner Seite
schlief, auf die eine und die andere Wange: "Was, du
wirst mir gar ins Gesicht scheissen?"

In diesen beiden Träumen treten an Stelle des
Teufels andere unheimliche Gestalten auf, Gespenster nämlich, als Geister Verstorbener. Der
Geist im zweiten Traum führt den Träumer selbst
auf den Friedhof, wo er mit der Kotentleerung ein
bestimmtes Grab bezeichnen soll. Ein Teil dieser
Situation ist nun sehr leicht zu verstehen. Der
Schläfer weiss, dass das Bett nicht der geeignete
Ort für die Befriedigung seines Bedürfnisses ist;
er lässt sich also im Traum von diesem wegführen
und er schafft sich eine Person, die seinem dunk-
len Drange den rechten Weg zeigt zu dem anderen

Ort, wo die Befriedigung des Bedürfnisses gestattet, ja durch die Umstände geboten ist. Der Geist im zweiten Traum bedient sich sogar bei dieser Führung einer Kerze, wie es ein Hausdiener thun würde, der den Fremden im Dunkel der Nacht zum W.C. geleitet. Warum sind aber diese Repräsentanten des Triebes zur Ortsveränderung, die sich der bequeme Schläfer durchaus ersparen will, so unheimliche Gesellen wie Gespenster und Geister von Verstorbenen, warum führt der Geist im zweiten Traum auf einen Friedhof wie zur Schändung eines Grabes? Diese Elemente scheinen doch mit dem Drang zur Kotentleerung und der Symbolisirung des Kotes durch Gold nichts zu thun haben. Es zeigt sich in ihnen ein Hinweis auf eine Angst, die man etwa auf ein Bemühen die Befriedigung im Bett zu unterdrücken, zurückführen könnte, ohne dass diese Angst gerade den spezifischen Charakter des auf den Tot hindeutenden Trauminhaltes erklärte. Wir enthalten uns hier noch der Deutung und heben ferner als erklärungsbedürftig hervor, dass in diesen beiden Situationen, wo zwei Männer mit einander schlafen, das unheimliche des gespenstischen Führers mit einem Weib in Zusammenhang gebracht ist. Der Geist des ersten Traumes enthüllt sich bald als eine schöne Frau, die sich nun erlöst fühlt, und der Geist des zweiten Traumes nimmt zum Ziel

[87]

das Grab eines Mädchens welches mit der Kenn-
zeichnung versehen werden soll.

Wir wenden uns zur weiteren Aufklärung an
andere solche Defaekationsträume, in denen die
Schlafgenossen nicht mehr zwei Männern, sondern
Mann und Frau, ein Ehepaar sind. Die im Schlaf in
Folge des Traumes vollzogene Befriedigungshand-
lung erscheint hier besonders abstossend, verbirgt
aber vielleicht gerade darum einen besonderen
Sinn.

Wir schicken hier seiner inhaltlichen Beziehun-
gen zu den nachstehenden einen Traum voraus,
der strenge genommen obiger Ankündigung nicht
entspricht. Er ist insoferne unvollständig, als die
Beschmutzung der Bettgenossin und Ehegattin
entfällt. Dafür ist der Zusammenhang des Defae-
kationsdranges mit der Todesangst überdeutlich.
Der Bauer, der als verheiratet bezeichnet ist,
träumt, dass er vom Blitze erschlagen wird, und
dass seine Seele zum Himmel schwebt. Oben bittet
er noch einmal zur Erde zurückkehren zu dürfen,
um Frau und Kinder zu sehen, bekommt die
Erlaubnis, sich in eine Spinne zu verwandeln und
sich an dem selbst gesponnenen Faden herabzu-
lassen. Der Faden wird zu kurz und im Bestreben,
noch mehr vom Faden aus seinem Leib herauszu-
drücken, erfolgt die Kotentleerung.

Anthr. VI. S.431, No. 9 Skatologische Erzählungen
aus Preussisch-Schlesien von Dr. von Waldheim.

Traum und Wirklichkeit.

Ein Bauer lag im Bett und träumte. Er sah sich auf
dem Felde bei seinen Ochsen und ackerte. Da fuhr
plötzlich ein Blitz hernieder und erschlug ihn. Nun
fühlte er deutlich, wie seine Seele nach oben schwebte
und auch schliesslich im Himmel ankam. Petrus
stand an der Eingangstüre und wollte den Bauer ein-
fach hineinschicken. Dieser aber bat, noch einmal auf
die Erde hinunter zu dürfen, um sich von seiner
Frau und seinen Kindern wenigstens verabschieden
zu können. Petrus aber meinte, das ginge nicht, und
wer einmal im Himmel sei, den lasse man nicht wieder
auf die Welt. Jetzt weinte der Bauer und bat jämmer-
lich bis Petrus endlich nachgab. Es gab nämlich nur
eine Möglichkeit für den Bauern, die Seinen wiederzusehen, wenn ihn Petrus in ein Tier verwandelte
und hinabschickte. So wurde der Bauer zu einer
Spinne und spann einen langen Faden, an dem er sich
hinunterliess. Als er ungefähr in Schornsteinhöhe
über seinem Gehöfte angekommen war, und seine
Kinder schon auf der Wiese spielen sah, merkte er zu
seinem Schrecken, dass er nicht mehr weiter spinnen
könnte. Die Angst war natürlich gross, denn er wollte
doch gänzlich auf die Erde. Deshalb drückte und
drückte er, damit der Faden länger würde. Er drückte
aus Leibeskräften—da gab es einen Krach—und der
Bauer erwachte.—Ihm war während des Schlafes
etwas sehr Menschliches passiert.

[89]

Wir begegnen hier dem gesponnenen Faden als einem neuen Symbol des entleerten Kotes, während uns die Psychoanalyse zu dieser Symbolisirung kein Gegenstück liefert, sondern dem Faden eine andere symbolische Bedeutung zuweist. Dieser Widerspruch wird späterhin seine Erledigung finden.

Der nächste, reich ausgeschmückte und scharf pointirte Traum ist ein sozusagen "geselliger"; er geht in die Beschmutzung der Ehefrau aus. Seine Übereinstimmungen mit dem vorstehenden Traum sind aber ganz auffällige. Der Bauer ist zwar nicht gestorben, aber er befindet sich im Himmel, will zur Erde zurückkehren, und verspürt die gleiche Verlegenheit, einen genug langen Faden zu "spinnen", an dem er sich herablassen kann. Diesen Faden schafft er sich aber nicht als Spinne aus seinem Körper, sondern in weniger phantastischer Weise aus allem, was er zusammenknüpfen kann, und wie der Faden noch immer nicht reicht, raten ihm die Englein direkt zu scheissen, um den Strick durch den Dreck zu verlängern.

"Geschlechtsleben des ukrainischen Bauernvolkes"
S196 *Des Bauern Himmelfahrt*

Ein Bauer träumte folgendes: Er hatte erfahren, dass im Himmel der Weizen in hohem Preise steht.

Da kriegte er Lust, seinen Weizen dorthin zu fahren.
Er belud seinen Wagen, spannte das Pferd ein und
machte sich auf den Weg. Er fuhr weit dahin, erblickte die Himmelstrasse und lenkte hin. So kam er
an das Himmeltor, und sieh da, es stand offen. Er
nahm einen direkten Anlauf, um stracks hineinzu-
fahren,—kaum hatte er aber den Wagen hingelenkt,
—schwups, da krachte das Tor zu. Da begann er zu
bitten: "Lasst mich hinein, seid so gut." Die Engel
aber liessen ihn nicht hinein, sagten, er habe sich ver-
spätet. Da sah er ein, dass hier kein Geschäft zu
machen sei,—es war ihm halt nicht beschieden und so
kehrte er um. Doch sieh' da. Der Weg war verschwun-
den, den er gefahren. Was sollte er da machen? Er
wandte sich wieder an die Engel: "Täubchen seid so
gut, führt mich zur Erde zurück, wenn's möglich ist,
gebt mir einen Weg, damit ich mit dem Gefährt nach
Hause gelange." Die Engel aber sagten: "Nein, Menschenkind, dein Gefährt bleibt hier, und du fahre
hinunter wie du willst."—"Wei werde ich mich da
hinablassen, hab' keinen Strick."—"Such nur etwas,
womit du dich hinablassen könntest." So nahm er halt
die Zügel, den Halfter, den Zaum, knüpfte alles an
einander und begann sich hinabzulassen; er kroch
und kroch, blickte hinunter, es fehlte noch viel bis
zur Erde. Er kroch wieder zurück und verlängerte das
Geknüpfte noch mit dem Gurt und Rüchenriemen.
Nun begann er wieder hinabzuklettern und es langte
noch immer nicht hinab zur Erde. Er knüpfte dann
die Deichsel mit dem Wagengestell (?) an, es war noch
zu kurz. Was war da zu tun? Er sann hin und her
und dann meinte er: "Na, ich wills noch mit dem

Rock, mit den Hosen, mit dem Hemd und obendrein mit dem Hosenband verlängern." So machte er's auch, knüpfte alles zusammen und kletterte weiter. Am Ende des Hosenbandes angelangt, war es noch immer weit zur Erde. Nun wusste er nicht, was er machen sollte; er hatte nichts mehr zum Weiteranknüpfen, und hinabzuspringen war's gefährlich, er konnte sich das Genick brechen. Bat er wieder die Engel: "Seid so gut, führt mich zur Erde." Die Engel sagten: "Scheiss und aus dem Dreck wird ein Strick."
—Er schiss und schiss beinahe eine halbe Stunde bis er nicht mehr womit zu scheissen hatte (bis er fertig war). Es ward daraus ein langer Strick und er kletterte an ihm hinab. Er kletterte und kletterte und gelangte an das Ende des Strickes, zur Erde aber war's noch immer weit. Da begann er wieder die Engel zu bitten, sie möchten ihn zur Erde bringen. Die Engel aber sagten: "Nun, jetzt, Menschenkind, brunze und daraus wird eine Seidenschnur." Der Bauer brunzte, brunzte immer fort bis er nicht mehr konnte. Er sah, dass daraus wahrhaftig eine Seidenschnur geworden und er kletterte weiter. Er kletterte und kletterte und gelangte an's Ende, sieh' da, es reichte zur Erde nicht, es fehlten noch 1½—2 Klafter. Er bat die Engel wieder, ihn hinabzuführen. Die Engel aber sagten: "Nein Bruder, jetzt ist dir nicht zu helfen, jetzt spring nur hinunter." Der Bauer zappelte unentschlossen, fand nicht den Mut hinabzuspringen, dann aber sah er ein, dass ihm kein anderer Ausweg blieb und plumps; statt vom Himmel flog er vom Ofen herunter und kam erst mitten in der Stube zur Besinnung. Da wachte er auf und rief: "Weib, Weib, wo bist du?"—

Das Weib wachte auf, sie hatte das Gepolter gehört und sagte: "Pfui Teufel über dich, bist du verrückt geworden?" Tastete um sich herum und sah die Bescherung: ihr Mann hatte sie ganz beschissen und bebrunzt. Sie begann zu schimpfen und ihm ordentlich den Kopf zu waschen. Der Bauer sagte: "Was schreist du? Es ist ohnehin ein Verdruss. Das Pferd ist verloren, im Himmel geblieben und ich wäre bald auch zu Grunde gegangen. Sag', Gott sei Dank, dass ich wenigstens am Leben geblieben."—"Was schwatzt du da, du bist ganz übergeschnappt; das Pferd ist im Stall und du warst auf dem Ofen, hast mich ganz besudelt und bist dann hinabgesprungen." Da fasste sich der Mann, erst jetzt ging ihm ein Licht auf, dass er alles bloss geträumt und dann erzählte er seinem Weibe den Traum, wie er in den Himmel fuhr und wie er von dort wieder zur Erde gelangte.

Hier drängt uns aber die Psychoanalyse eine Deutung auf, welche die ganze Auffassung dieser Gattung von Träumen verändert. Gegenstände, die sich verlängern, sagt uns die Erfahrung der Traumdeutung, sind durchwegs Symbole für die Erektion.* In diesen beiden Schwankträumen liegt der Akzent auf dem Element, dass der Faden nicht lang genug werden will, und auch die Angst ist im

---

* [Randbemerkung, E. O.]. In einer Geschichte aus der Picardie dient als symb. Abbild der Erektion die Verschiebung eines Fingerringes nach abwärts. Je tiefer der Ring sinkt, desto länger—die Analogie wirkt natürlich zaubermächtig—wird der Penis. (Krypt. I N. 32)

Traume gerade daran geknüpft. Der Faden ist überdiess wie alle seine Analoga (Strick, Seil, Zwirn etc.) ein Symbol des Samens.* Der Bauer bemüht sich also, eine Erektion zu Stande zu bringen, und erst als diess nicht gelingt, wendet er sich zur Kotentleerung. Hinter der exkrementellen Not dieser Träume kommt mit einem Male die sexuelle Not zum Vorschein.

Diese eignet sich aber auch viel besser dazu, die übrigen Inhaltsbestandteile des Traumes zu erklären. Man muss sich sagen, wenn wir annehmen wollen, diese erfundenen Träume seien im Wesentlichen korrekt gebildet, so kann die Traumhandlung, in der sie enden, nur eine sinnvolle und von den latenten Gedanken des Träumers beabsichtigte sein. Wenn der Träumer am Ende sein Eheweib bekackt so muss der ganze Traum dahin zielen und diesen Effekt motiviren. Er kann nichts anderes bedeuten, als eine Schmähung, strenge genommen, eine Verschmähung des Weibes. Mit dieser liesse sich dann die tiefere Bedeutung der im Traume ausgedrückten Angst leicht in Verbindung bringen.

Die Situation aus welcher dieser letzte Traum erwächst, können wir nach diesen Andeutungen in folgender Art konstruiren. Den Schläfer über-

---

* Vgl. *Stekel* Die Sprache des Traumes 1911.

[94]

fällt ein starkes erotisches Bedürfnis, welches im Eingang des Traumes in ziemlich deutlichen Symbolen angezeigt ist (Er hat gehört, dass der Weizen [wol gleich Samen] hoch im Preise steht. Er nimmt einen Anlauf, um mit Pferd und Wagen [Genitalsymbole] ins offene Himmelstor einzufahren.) Aber diese libidinöse Regung gilt wahrscheinlich einem nicht erreichbaren Objekt. Das Tor schliesst sich, er giebt die Absicht auf und will zur Erde zurückkehren. Das Eheweib, das nahe bei ihm ruht, reizt ihn aber nicht; er bemüht sich vergebens, für sie eine Erektion zu haben. Der Wunsch, sie zu beseitigen, um sie durch eine andere und bessere zu ersetzen, ist im infantilen Sinne ein Todeswunsch. Wer solche Wünsche im Unbewussten gegen eine eigentlich doch geliebte Person hegt, dem wandeln sie sich in Todesangst, Angst um das eigene Leben. Daher in diesen Träumen das Gestorbensein, die Himmelfahrt, die heuchlerische Sehnsucht, Weib und Kinder wiederzusehen. Die enttäuschte sexuelle Libido aber lässt sich auf dem Wege der Regression durch die exkrementelle Wunschregung ablösen welche das untaugliche Sexualobjekt beschimpft und besudelt.

Wenn uns dieser eine Traum eine solche Deutung nahelegt, so kann deren Erweis unter Rücksicht auf die Eigentümlichkeiten des vorliegenden

Materials nur gelingen, indem wir dieselbe Deutung auf eine ganze Reihe von inhaltlich verwandten Träumen anwenden. Greifen wir in dieser Absicht auf die früher erwähnten Träume der Situation zurück, dass der Schläfer einen Mann zum Bettgenossen hat. Dann wird uns nachträglich die Beziehung bedeutungsvoll, in welcher das Weib in diesen Träumen auftritt. Der Schläfer, von einer libidinösen Regung befallen, verschmäht den Mann, er wünscht ihn weit weg und ein Weib an seine Stelle. Der Todeswunsch gegen den unerwünschten Bettgenossen wird von der moralischen Zensur natürlich nicht so schwer gestraft wie der gegen die Ehefrau, aber die Reaktion reicht doch hin, um ihn gegen die eigene Person, oder auf das erwünschte weibliche Objekt zu wenden. Der Schläfer wird selbst vom Tode geholt, nicht der Mann, sondern das ersehnte Weib ist verstorben. Am Ende aber bricht sich die Verschmähung des männlichen Sexualobjektes in der Besudelung Bahn, und diese wird auch vom anderen wie eine Beschimpfung empfunden und geahndet.

Unsere Deutung passt also für diese Gruppe von Träumen. Wenn wir nun zu den Träumen mit Besudelung der Frau zurückkehren, so sind wir darauf vorbereitet, dass wir das an dem Mustertraum vermisste oder nur angedeutete in anderen ähnlichen Träumen unverkennbar ausgedrückt finden werden.

[96]

Im folgenden Defaekationstraum ist die Beschmutzung der Frau nicht betont, aber mit aller Deutlichkeit, soweit es auf symbolischem Wege geschehen kann, ist gesagt, dass die libidinöse Regung einer anderen Frau gilt. Der Träumer will nicht seinen eigenen Acker beschmutzen, sondern will zur Defaekation auf das Feld das Nachbarn.

Anthrop. Bd. IV. Deutsche Bauernerzählungen. Gesammelt im Ober- und Unter-Elsass von F. Wernert. S. 138 No. 173

Du Stück Vieh.

Ein Bauer träumte, auf dem Kleeacker bei der Arbeit zu sein. Darüber kam ihm harte Not an und da er seinen Klee nicht verdrecken wollte eilte er an den im Nachbarstück stehenden Baum, riss die Hosen runter und schmetterte einen Fladen Numero Pfiff auf den Boden. Endlich wie er mit Genuss fertig war, will er sich auch säubern und beginnt, kräftig Gras abzurupfen. Aber was war denn das? Jählings fuhr unser Bäuerlein aus dem Schlafe auf und hielt sich seine schwerzend brennende Wange an die es eben geklatscht hatte. "Du taub stickel Vieh", hört da der zu sich kommende Bauer dessen Weib neben ihm im Bett poltern, "bruchsch m'r au noch d'Hoor volls (-vollends) vum Lieb (-Leib) hinweg ropfe."

Das Ausrupfen der Haare (des Grases), welches hier die Stelle* der Besudelung einnimmt, findet sich im nächsten Traume neben derselben er-

---

* [An dieser Stelle ist am Rand ein Fragezeichen von E. O.]

wähnt. Die psychoanalytische Erfahrung zeigt, dass es aus dem Symbolkreis der Onanie (ausreissen, abreissen) stammt.

Der Unterstützung am ehesten bedürftig erschiene in unserer Deutung der Todeswunsch des Träumers gegen sein Weib. Aber in dem nun mitzutheilenden Traum begräbt der Träumer direkt sein, heuchlerisch als Schatz bezeichnetes— Weib, indem er das Gefäss, welches das Gold enthält in die Erde eingräbt und wie wir es in den Schatzträumen gewohnt waren, den Kothaufen als Zeichen darauf pflanzt. Während des Grabens arbeitet er mit den Händen in der Vagina seiner Frau.*

Anthrop. V. Schwänke und Schnurren niederösterreichischer Landleute. Von. A. Riedl No. 19 (S. 140)

Der Traum vom Schatz.

A Baua hat amal an fürchtalichen Tram ghabt. 'S is eahm grad virkömma, als obs Kriagzeit wa' und de ganze Gegend vo de feindlichn Soldatn plindert wurt. Er hat awa an Schatz ghabt, um den eahm so baung war, das er gar net recht aus und ei' damit gewisst hat und wo - er - a 'n eigentli vastecken soll. Endli kummt a drauf, das a 'n sein' Gartn vagrabt, wo - r - a a recht a schens Platzi gewusst hat. No also, es tramt eahm

---

* [Randbemerkung, E. O.] Bedeutung?

halt weida, wie - r - a just aussigeht und zu den Platzl kummt, wo - r - a d' Erde aufgrabn wüll, damit a den grossen Kruach ins Loch einestelln kaun. Wie - r - a awa so nach an Grabscheit suacht, findt a rundemadum ni und muass schliessli d' Händ dazua nehma. Er macht also's Loch mit de blossn Händ, stellt 'n Plutza mit 'n Geld eini und schitt das Gaunzi wieda mit Erdn zua. Hiatz will a geh, bleibt awa nomal steh und denkt si: "Waun awa d' Soldatn wieda weg san, wia wir' i daun mein Schatz findn, waun i net a Zoacha hintua?" Und glei fängt a ins Suachn an, suacht ibarall, obn, unt, hint und vurn, wo - r - a nut kaum, ja er findt halt nirgands nix, damit a glei immer wusst, wo - r - a sei Geld vagrabn hat. No, da kummt eahm awa grad d' Not au. "A", sagt a zu eahm seba, " 'S is a so a guat, waun i drauf scheiss." Ziagt natirli d' Hosen glei und macht an recht an trum Haufn auf de Stell, w - r - a 'n Plutza rinigstellt hat. Drauf siacht a danebn a Bischl Gras und will 's ausreissn, damit a si awischn kann. Den Moment kriagt a awa so a trum Watschn, das a augnblickli munta wird und gaunzt vaduzt dreiguckt. Und glei drauf hert a, wia 'n sei Weib, das gaunz aus 'n Häusl is, anbrüllt: "Du Patznlippl, Du elendiga, glaubst i muass ma allas von Dir gfalln lassn? Z'erscht stierst ma mit Deine zwa Händ in da Fumml um, daun scheisst ma drauf und hiatz willst ma gar no d'Haar a davo ausreissn."

Wir sind mit diesem Traumbeispiel wieder zu den Schatzträumen zurückgekehrt, von denen wir ausgegangen sind, und bemerken, dass jene, Defaekationsträume, die von einem Schatz handeln,

[99]

nichts oder wenig von Todesangst enthalten, wogegen die anderen, in denen die Todesbeziehung direkt ausgesprochen ist (Himmelfahrtsträume) vom Schatze absehen und die Defaekation anders motiviren. Es ist beinahe, als ob die heuchlerische* Verwandlung des Weibes in einen Schatz die Bestrafung für den Todeswunsch erspart hätte.

Am deutlichsten wird der Todeswunsch gegen das Weib in einem anderen Himmelfahrtstraum eingestanden, der aber nicht in eine Defaekation auf den Körper des Weibes, sondern in eine sexuelle Vornahme an ihren Genitalien, wie schon im vorigen Traum ausgeht. Der Träumer verkürzt direkt das Leben des Weibes, um seines zu verlängern, indem er Öl aus ihrer Lebenslampe in die seinige thut. Wie zum Ersatz für diese unverhohlene Feindseligkeit tritt zum Schlusse des Traumes etwas wie ein Versuch einer Liebkosung auf.

Anthr. IV. S. 255. No. 10:
Das Lebenslicht.

Erzählt von einem Gymnasiallehrer in Belgrad nach der Mitteilung einer Bäuerin aus der Gegend von Kragujevac.

Der heilige Petrus erschien einem Manne, als der fest eingeschlafen war und führte ihn ins Paradies

---

* [Randbemerkung, von E. O., der "heuchlerische" unterstrichen hat.] ? Aber Schatz d. Traum des einen Schlafgenossen.

weg. Von Herzen gern willigte der Mann ein und
ging mit dem heiligen Petrus. Lange irrten sie im
Paradies umher und kamen zu einem grossen und
geräumigen, dabei sehr schön in Ordnung gehaltenen
Wäldchen, allwo auf jedem Baume mehrere Hängelampen brannten. Der Mann fragte den heiligen
Petrus, was das hier bedeuten solle. Der heilige Petrus
antwortete, das wären Hängelampen, die nur solange
brannten, als da der Mensch lebe, sowie jedoch das
Oel verschwände und die Hängelampe verlösche,
müsste auch der Mensch sofort versterben. Das hat
den sehr interessiert und er bat den heiligen Petrus,
er möge ihn zu seiner Hängelampe hinführen. Der
heilige Petrus erhörte die Bitte und geleitete ihn zur
Hängelampe seines Weibes hin und gleich dabei be-
fand sich auch die des Mannes. Der Mann sah, dass in
der Hängelampe des Weibes noch viel Oel vorhanden
war, in seiner eigenen aber sehr wenig und es tat ihm
sehr leid, weil er bald sterben müsste und da bat er
den heiligen Petrus, er möchte noch ein wenig Oel in
seine Hängelampe zugiessen. Der heilige Petrus sagte,
Gott schütte da Oel gleich bei der Geburt eines
Menschen ein und bestimme jedem die Lebensdauer.
Das versetzte den Mann in trübe Stimmung und er
jammerte neben der Hängelampe. Der heilige Petrus
sprach zu ihm: "Bleib du jetzt da, ich aber muss
weiter gehen, ich habe noch zu tun." Der Mann freute
sich dessen und kaum rückte der heilige Petrus aus
der Sehweite, begann er den Finger in seines Weibes
Hängelampe einzutunken und in seine das Oel einzu-
tröpfeln. So tat er es mehrmals und sobald als der
heilige Petrus nahte, fuhr er zusammen, erschrak und

erwachte davon und da merkte er, dass er den Finger in des Weibes Voz eingetunkt und leckend in seinen Mund den Finger abgeträufelt habe.

Anmerkung.* Nach einer von einem Handwerker in Sarajevo erzählten Fassung erwachte der Mann nach einer Ohrfeige seiner Ehegattin, die er mit dem Herumbohren in ihrer Scham aufgeweckt. Hier fehlt der heilige Petrus und statt der Hängelampen brennen Gläser mit Oel. Nach einer dritten Fassung, die ich von einem Schüler aus Mostar erfahren, zeigt ein ehrwürdiger Greis dem Manne verschiedene brennende Kerzen. Seine ist sehr dünn, die des Weibes riesig dick. Nun beginnt der Mann, um sein Leben zu verlängern, mit brennendem Eifer die dicke Kerze zu belecken. Da kriegt er aber eine gewaltige Watschen. Dass du ein Vieh bist, das wusste ich, doch dass du ein Ferkel bist, das wusste ich wahrhaftig nicht, sagte sein Weib zu ihm, da er im Schlaf die Voze beleckte.

Die Geschichte ist ausserordentlich weit in Europa verbreitet.

Es ist jetzt an der Zeit, uns an den "bösen Traum" jener Frau zu erinnern, die am Ende ihren Manne am Gliede zog, als ob sie es ausreissen wollte. Die Deutung, zu welcher wir uns dort veranlasst sahen, stimmt mit der hier vertretenen Deutung der Defaekationsträume des Mannes völlig zusammen. Aber auch der Traum

---

* [Randbemerkung, E. O.] Kryptadia V. S. 15 (ganz ähnlich aus der *Ukraine*)

der unbefriedigten Frau schafft den Mann (und das Kind) als Hindernis für die Befriedigung ungeniert bei Seite.

Ein anderer Defaekationstraum, dessen Deutung vielleicht keine volle Sicherheit gestattet, mahnt uns doch, eine gewisse Abänderung in der Absicht dieser Träume zuzulassen, und wirft ein neues Licht auf Träume wie die letzterwähnten und einige noch mitzutheilende, in denen die Traumhandlung in einer Manipulation an den Genitalien des Weibes besteht.

Anthrop. V
Südslavische Volksüberlieferungen, die sich auf den Geschlechtsverkehr beziehen. Von Dr. Friedr.
S. Krauss
S. 293 No. 697:

Vor Schrecken.

Der Pascha nächtigte beim Begen. Als der Morgen tagte, da lag noch der Beg und mochte nicht aufstehen. Fragt der Beg den Pascha: "Was hat dir geträumt?"—"Ich träumte, auf dem Minaret wäre noch ein Minaret gewesen."—"Uf, das wäre," wundert sich der Beg. "Und was hast du noch geträumt?" —"Ich träumte," sagt er, "auf diesem Minaret stünde ein Kupferbecken, im Becken aber wäre Wasser. Der Wind weht, das Kupferbecken wiegt sich. Ja, was hättest du getan, wenn du dies geträumt hättest?"— "Ich hätte mich vor Schrecken sowohl bepisst als beschissen."—"Und siehst du, ich habe mich bloss bepisst."

Eine Aufforderung zur symbolischen Deutung dieses Traumes liegt darin, dass sein manifester Inhalt recht unverständlich, die Symbole aber eher aufdringlich klar sind. Warum sollte der Träumer eigentlich erschrecken, wenn er ein Wasserbecken sich auf der Spitze eines Minarets wiegen sieht? Ein Minaret ist aber vortrefflich zum Symbol des Penis geeignet, und das rythmisch bewegte Wassergefäss scheint ein gutes Symbol des weiblichen Genitales im Coitusakte. Der Pascha hat also einen Coitustraum gehabt und wenn ihm von seinem Gastgeber zugemutet wird, dabei zu defaeziren, so liegt es nahe die Deutung darin zu suchen, dass beide alte und impotente Männer sind, bei denen das Alter dieselbe sprichwörtliche Ersetzung der Geschlechtslust durch die exkrementelle Lust hervorgerufen hat, die wir in den anderen Träumen durch die Versagung des geeigneten Sexualobjektes entstanden sahen. Wer nicht mehr koitieren kann, meint das Volk in seiner derben Wahrheitsliebe, dem bliebt noch das Vergnügen am Scheissen; bei dem, können wir sagen kommt die Analerotik wieder zum Vorschein, die früher da war als die Genitalerotik, und durch diese jüngere Regung verdrängt und abgelöst wurde. Die Defaekationsträume konnten also auch Impotenzträume sein.

Die Abänderung der Deutung ist nicht so erheblich, wie es auf den ersten Blick scheinen könnte. Auch bei den Defaekationsträumen, deren Opfer das Weib wird, handelt es sich um Impotenz, relative Impotenz allerdings gegen die eine Person, welche ihren Reiz für den Träumer eingebüsst hat. Der Defaekationstraum wird so zum Traum des Mannes, der das Weib nicht mehr befriedigen kann, wie jenes Mannes, den ein Weib nicht mehr befriedigt.

Die nämliche Deutung als Impotenztraum lässt nun auch ein Traum in den Facetien des *Poggio* zu, der sich manifest allerdings als der Traum eines Eifersüchtigen gebärdet, also doch eines Mannes, der seiner Frau nicht zu genügen vermeint.

Poggio: Facetien N.133 S.105 der Übersetzung von Alfred Semeran (Bd. IV von "Romanische Meistererzähler" herausgegeb. v. F. S. Krauss)

Der Ring der Treue

Franciscus Philelphus war eifersüchtig auf sein Weib und wurde von der grössten Sorge gequält, dass sie es mit einem anderen Mann hielte u. Tag u. Nacht lag er auf der Lauer. Da uns nun im Traume wiederzukehren pflegt, was uns im Wachen beschäftigt, so erschien ihm während seines Schlummers ein Dämon, der sagte ihm, wenn er nach seinem Geheiss täte, würde ihm sein Weib ewig die Treue halten.

Franciscus sagte es ihm im Traume zu, er würde ihm sehr dankbar sein u. versprach ihm eine Belohnung.

"Nimm den Ring da," erwiderte der Dämon, "und trag ihn sorgfältig am Finger. So lang du ihn trägst, kann Dein Weib mit keinem anderen zusammenliegen, ohne dass du es weisst."

Wie er froh erregt aufwachte, fühlte er dass sein Finger in der vulva seiner Frau stecke.

Ein besseres Mittel haben die Eifersüchtigen nicht, so können ihre Weiber nie ohne Wissen der Männer sich von einem anderen vornehmen lassen.

Als Quelle dieses Schwankes von *Poggio* gilt eine Erzälung die *Rabelais,* die sonst sehr ähnlich, insoferne deutlicher ist, als sie den Ehemann direkt auf seine alten Tage ein junges Weib heimführen lässt, die ihm nun Grund zu eifersüchtigen Befürchtungen giebt.

Rabelais: Pantagruel, Buch II. cap. 28, S.139. der Übersetzung von Hegaur u. Owlglass

"Hans Carvel war ein gelehrter, erfahrener, fleissiger Mann, ein Ehrenmann von gutem Verstand und Urteil, wohlwollend, barmherzig gegen die Armen und ein heiterer Philosoph; zu allem ein wackerer Kumpan, der gern seine Spässe machte, ein bischen wohlbeleibt allerdings und wackelköpfig, aber sonst

in allewege gut bei einander. Auf seine alten Tage
ehelichte er die Tochter des Amtmanns Concordat,
ein junges, dralles, artiges, munteres und gefälliges
Weiblein, bloss eben ein wenig sehr freundlich gegen
die Herren Nachbarn und Hausknechte. So kam's,
dass er im Verlaufe etlicher Wochen eifersüchtig
ward wie ein Tiger und argwöhnte, sie möchte sich
eines Tages in einer fremden Werkstatt besohlen
lassen. Um dem vorzubauen, erzählt' er ihr einen
ganzen Schock schöner Historien von den Strafen des
Ehebruchs, las ihr oft liebliche Legenden von sitt-
samen Frauen vor, predigt' ihr das Evangelium der
Keuschheit, schrieb ihr ein Büchlein Lobgesänge auf
die eheliche Treue, tadelte mit scharfen und ein-
dringlichen Worten die Lüderlichkeit unzüchtiger
Eheweiber und schenkt' ihr obendrein noch ein
prächtiges Halsband, das rings mit orientalischen
Saphiren besetzt war.

Aber dessen ohngeachtet sah er sie also freundlich
und zutunlich mit den Nachbarn umgehen, dass seine
Eifersucht nur immer mehr anstieg. In einer Nacht
nun, da er in so leidvollen Gedanken mit ihr zu Bett
lag, träumt' ihm, er spreche mit dem Leibhaftigen
und klage ihm seinen Kummer. Aber der Teufel
tröstet' ihn, steckt' ihm einen Ring an den Finger
und sprach: "Nimm hier diesen Ring; solang du ihn
am Finger trägst, wird dein Weib ohne dein Wissen
und Wollen von keinem anderen fleischlich erkannt
werden."—"Viel tausend Dank, Herr Teufel," sagte
Hans Carvel. "Ich will Mahomet verleugnen, wenn
ich je den Ring vom Finger ziehe." Der Teufel ver-
schwand; Hans Carvel aber erwachte frohen Herzens

und fand, dass er den Finger in seiner Frau Wie-
heisstsdochgleich hatte.

Ich vergass zu erzählen, wie das Weiblein, da sie's
verspürte, mit dem Steiss nach hinten bockte, als
wollt' sie sagen: "Halt, nein—nein, da herein gehört
was anderes", was den Hans Carvel bedeucht', als
wollt' man ihm seinen Ring abziehen.

Ist das kein unfehlbar Mittel? Glaub' mir, handle
nach diesem Vorbild und trag' Sorge, allzeit deines
Weibes Ring am Finger zu haben."*

Der Teufel, der wie in den Schatzträumen hier
als Ratgeber auftritt, lässt wol einiges von den
latenten Gedanken des Träumers erraten. Er
sollte wol ursprünglich das ungetreue, schwer zu
bewachende Weib "holen";** er zeigt dann im
manifesten Traum das unfehlbare Mittel, wie man
es dauernd bewahren kann. Auch hierin erkennen
wir eine Analogie mit dem Beseitigungs- (Todes-)
Wunsch der Defaekationsträume.

---

* [Fussnote von Freud.] Auf diese Symbolik des Ringes und
des Fingers bezieht sich *Goethe* in einem venetianischen Epigram (Nr 65 der Paralipomena. Sophienausgabe, 5 Bd. II.
p. 381).

"Köstliche Ringe besitz ich! Gegrabne fürtreffliche Steine
Hoher Gedanken und Styls fasset ein lauteres Gold.
Theuer bezahlt man die Ringe geschmückt mit feurigen Steinen
Blinken hast du sie oft über dem Spieltisch gesehen.
Aber ein Ringelchen kenn ich, das hat sich anders gewaschen
Das Hans Carvel einmal traurig im Alter besass.
Unklug schob er den kleinsten der zehen Finger ins Ringchen,
Nur der grösste gehört würdig, der eilfte, hinein."

** [Am Rand ein Fragezeichen von E. O.]

Wir wollen diese kleine Sammlung beschliessen, indem wir in lockerem Zusammenhange einen Lotterietraum anfügen, welcher unsere vorhin geäusserte Vermutung, die Lotterie symbolisiere die Eheschliessung, unterstützen kann.

Geschlechtsleben des ukrainischen Bauernvolkes.

S. 40 *Es gab eine Reue, doch gab's kein Zurück.*

Ein Kaufmann hatte einen wunderlichen Traum. Er träumte, dass er einen weiblichen Arsch mit allem Zugehör gesehen. Auf der einen Hälfte stand die Ziffer 1, auf der zweiten 3. Der Kaufmann hatte noch vorher im Sinne, ein Lotterielos zu kaufen. Dieses Traumbild deucht ihm eine Glückverkündigung. Ohne die neunte Stunde abzuwarten, lief er gleich in der Früh in's Bankgeschäft, um das Los zu kaufen. Er kam dort an und ohne sich lange zu besinnen, verlangte er das Los No. 13 diejenigen Zahlen, die er im Traume gesehen. Nachdem er das Los gekauft, verging kein Tag, an dem er nicht in allen Zeitungen nachgesehen hätte, ob sein Los gewonnen. Nach einer Woche, nein spätestens nach etwa anderthalb, bekommt man die Ziehungsliste. Wie er nun nachschaut, sieht er, dass seine Nummer nicht gezogen worden, wohl aber die Nummer 103, Serie 8, und die gewann 200000 Rubel. Der Kaufmann hätte sich beinahe die Haare ausgerauft. "Ich muss mich wohl geirrt haben, es ist etwas nicht richtig." Er war ganz aus dem Häuschen, er ward beinahe trübsinnig und begriff nicht, was das bedeutete, dass er so einen

Traum gesehen. Dann beschloss er mit seinem Freunde die Sache zu erörtern, ob dieser ihm nicht (das Pech) erklären könnte. Er begegnete dem Freunde, erzählte ihm alles haarklein. Da sagte der Freund: "Ach, du Einfaltpinsel. Hast du denn nicht am Arsch zwischen der Nummer 1 und 3 die Null bemerkt? . . ."—"A-a-ah, der Teufel hol's, ich bin gar nicht darauf verfallen, dass der Arsch die Null vorstellte."—"Aber es war doch ganz klar und deutlich, du hast nur nicht die Losnummer richtig herausgefunden, und die Nummer 8 der Serie—das stellte dein Voz vor, die ist der Ziffer 8 ähnlich." Und es gab eine Reue, doch gab's kein Zurück.

Unsere Absicht bei der Abfassung dieser kleinen Arbeit war eine zweifache. Wir wollten einerseits mahnen, dass man sich durch die oft abstossend schmutzige und indezente Art des volkstümlichen Materials nicht abhalten lassen solle, in demselben nach wertvollen Bestätigungen für die psychoanalytischen Auffassungen zu suchen. So konnten wir diesmal feststellen, dass das Folklore Traumsymbole in der nämlichen Weise deutet wie die Psychoanalyse, und dass es im Gegensatz zu laut ausgesprochenen volkstümlichen Meinungen eine Gruppe von Träumen auf aktuell gewordene Bedürfnisse und Wünsche zurückführt. Anderseits möchten wir aussprechen, dass man dem Volke unrecht thut, wenn man annimmt, dass es diese Art der Unterhaltung nur zur Befriedigung der gröbsten Gelüste pflegt. Es scheint vielmehr, dass sich hinter diesen hässlichen Façaden seelische Reaktionen auf ernst zu nehmende, ja traurig stimmende Lebenseindrücke verbergen, denen sich der Mann aus dem Volke nur nicht ohne einen groben Lustgewinn hingeben will.